COSPLAY
WORLD

COSPLAY WORLD

Brian Ashcraft and Luke Plunkett

PRESTEL

MUNICH · LONDON · NEW YORK

Contents

Introduction

In March 1910 an unnamed woman in Tacoma, Washington, took first prize at a masquerade ball with a most unusual costume. Shortly afterwards, a friend of the woman, Mr Otto James, borrowed the suit. Hoping to advertise his ice-skating rink, he wore it down a busy Tacoma street, where turn-of-the-century police weren't quite ready for the spectacle. He was promptly arrested on charges of public masquerading, before being released on $10 bail.

The costume was so unusual because it was based not on a figure from myth or literature, but one from a newspaper comic strip. In 1907, cartoonist A. D. Condo created *Mr Skygack From Mars*, a bumbling Martian anthropologist who appeared for several years in newspapers across America and is credited as being the world's first science fiction comic star.

Mr Skygack costume sightings were soon being recorded across America, some as early as 1908. People had long been dressing up as characters, creatures and monsters for all kinds of reasons, but drastic changes were taking place around the time *Mr Skygack* first appeared. Unlike the heroes of books or legend, the advent of modern media –

comic books, print newspapers, film, TV and, later, video games – let fans actually see the characters they idolised, and in doing so copy their appearance.

As the 20th century marched on, through Buck Rogers and J.R.R. Tolkien, *Star Trek* and *Star Wars*, science fiction and fantasy works exploded into the mainstream. And as the ranks of the devoted increased, diehards began coming together to share exciting new ways to show their dedication. One such way was to dress up like their heroes.

Not that the rest of the world was aware of this – or could see what was coming. Even as recently as the late 1990s few outside Japan, where the actual word 'cosplay' was created, had ever heard the term. Those few who had might easily have written it off as a weird craze – some Japanese phenomenon that would soon die out.

But it didn't die out. Cosplay is now taking over. Comprising elements of costuming, performance art, acting and sometimes even marketing, 'cosplay' is now to dressing up as characters from pop culture what 'Coke' is to cola and 'Kleenex' is to tissues.

Once a haven for social outcasts and geek pioneers, cosplay is now a celebrated art form, one

An article about *Mr Skygack From Mars* costumes, in the *Spokane Press*, 19 December 1908.

that has spawned its own communities, magazines, specialist shops, TV programmes and even books. A lot has changed over the decades, but it is possible to see that as far back as *Mr Skygack*, without television or the Internet for help and guidance, the roots of modern cosplay were beginning to take hold. The homage to a character. The craftsmanship in making prize-winning costumes. The spectacle. The art of causing jaws to drop and wowing crowds, of transforming a person from someone who simply admires a character into someone who, at least for a moment, really is that character. And even, as in the case of Otto James, a touch of the absurd.

From humble beginnings at ice rinks and in jail cells to global advertising and TV shows, cosplay has come a long way. But as much as things have changed, and will continue to change, one thing will remain the same: cosplay is an expression of creativity and love. If only those early *Mr Skygack* fans could see the world of cosplay now. They'd fit right in.

Brian Ashcraft and Luke Plunkett, 2014

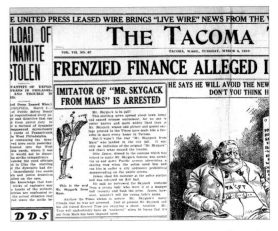

An article about Otto James's arrest due to his *Mr Skygack From Mars* costume from the *Tacoma Times*, 8 March 1910.

Forrest J. Ackerman and Myrtle R. Douglas in their original creations at the very first Worldcon in 1939.

Pierre Pettinger

HISTORIAN

While the simple act of dressing up as a character may be over a century old, many of the aspects fundamental to modern cosplay were actually inherited from a similar craft known as costuming, under whose wing cosplay would grow into what it has become today. 'The first World Science Fiction Convention [Worldcon] was held in New York in 1939,' says Pierre Pettinger, chief archivist of the International Costumers' Guild. Though this wasn't the first mass meeting of sci-fi fans – there had been earlier conventions held in Philadelphia and Britain – according to Pettinger it is the first recorded instance of anyone attending in a fancy outfit.

Two attendees, pioneering sci-fi fans Myrtle R. Douglas and Forrest J. Ackerman, turned up wearing 'futuristic costumes', both of which had been designed and constructed by Douglas. Ackerman would go on to be one of the founding fathers of modern science fiction, as a writer, editor and fan – indeed, he's credited with coining the term 'sci-fi' in 1954 – while Douglas helped spearhead the rise of sci-fi fanzines, or fan-made magazines. 'Ackerman's intent was to promote newspaper coverage of the event,' says Pettinger. 'That attempt was unsuccessful. But his example inspired many of the attendees.'

A year later, at the next Worldcon, in Chicago, several attendees brought their own costumes – enough that an impromptu exhibition took place. Later events would see these competitions formalised and a mainstay of the costuming scene, the masquerade, was born.

As for Pettinger himself, he and his wife Sandy (also a member of the Guild) became active in costuming in the early 1980s. 'That was the peak of Worldcon masquerades,' he says. 'After that, entries started to slow down. We are beginning to see some re-emergence in numbers, but it is still spotty.' Part of that re-emergence is thanks to the rising popularity of cosplay. 'Cosplayers are still somewhat young and enthusiastic . . . I can see them revitalising generic costuming and leading both to new heights.'

Douglas and Ackerman's pioneering appearance would help pave the way for generations of costumers to find each other, get together and share their art in a public space. What they couldn't have known at the time, though, was that the costuming scene they'd helped create would later pave the way for something even bigger.

Kathryn Mayer as Gwendolyn Novak from Robert A. Heinlein's sci-fi novel *The Cat who Walks through Walls* (1985).

Bruce Mai

HISTORIAN

Cosplay may have grown up under costuming's wing, but it now occupies its own space on the cultural landscape. Bruce Mai from the International Costumers' Guild remembers a time when the act of dressing up as a character was known by a different term.

The costuming scene evolved as a way for people to dress creatively and in an outlandish fashion. But while most would come up with their own original outfits, as the 20th century moved on, more and more costumers began to pay homage to popular characters from books, movies, TV and comics. 'Character tributes are commonly referred to as "recreations" in the broader costuming community,' says Mai. The distinction he makes between what he sees as two separate fields is interesting and perhaps surprising. While having common ancestry, where modern cosplay usually involves dressing up as an existing character from a medium with a visual reference (such as comic books, films, animated series or video games), the definition of costuming is much looser, allowing not just for what we'd today consider cosplay but also fresh interpretations of literary characters, or even wholly original creations.

What began as 'recreation costuming', then, has since become so popular that it has outgrown its status as a niche within costuming and has spun off and developed into a pastime now widely recognised in its own right. 'There is still a lot of original costuming,' Mai says. 'However, recreations have become more common due to the proliferation of pop culture conventions and the wide accessibility of media sources. More of the general public recognises and accepts these people as "cosplayers".'

Mai believes today's popular consensus around the meaning of 'cosplay' – the act of dressing up in any kind of fantastic, fictional costume – to be erroneous, as it intrudes on ground costuming had occupied long before cosplay came into its own. The divide between the terms may seem trivial, but it's important to those still active in the costuming scene which, having been around since before the Second World War, enjoys a long and proud tradition.

Judith Miller as Captain Juditkah, an original creation, in the 1970s.

A cosplayer poses as Wonder Woman at a convention in the 1970s.

Ron Miller

PHOTOGRAPHER

'A costumer had covered himself with peanut butter and entered a masquerade as a turd. He was doing fine until, after several hours of hot lights, the peanut butter not only began to melt, but turned rancid.'

This might sound extreme, but so was costuming (and, by extension, the growing cosplay scene) in the 1970s in the United States. Things we'd these days consider too overtly sexy or outrageous to be seen on a stage were par for the course. Ron Miller, an acclaimed sci-fi illustrator and author, began documenting American costuming before most of today's cosplayers were born, taking photographs of conventions while his wife, an avid costumer at the time, won awards for her outfits. One of the things he remembers about those early costumes was, well, the occasional lack of costume. 'In many ways it's too bad that costuming has become so prudish! . . . One really good reason for nude cosplay at the time was that one of the prime goals of serious costumers is to recreate a character accurately, and many characters, like Dejah Thoris from Edgar Rice Burroughs's *Barsoom* novels, are described as being at least partially nude. There were only a scant handful of examples where a costumer employed nudity just for the sake of doing so,' says Miller. 'In almost every case I can think of, the nudity of a costume was accepted for what it was: a necessary part in the recreation of a character.'

But by the end of the decade, some costumers had begun to let things get out of hand and were showing skin just for the sake of it. Not only was this ruffling the feathers of members of the costuming community, but hotel ballrooms, where masquerade events were held, also had their own rules about public decency. As Miller explains, this led to the creation of the 'No Costume is No Costume' rule at most masquerades. Partial nudity was still allowed, however, as long as it was a legitimate part of a character recreation.

It's not just the amount of skin on show that's changed over the years, though. Miller also points out that many cosplayers' 'attention to accurate replication of a character does seem obsessive' and reminds us that, while outsiders might be less aware of it being part of the scene in recent decades, traditional costuming conventions still exist, and offer cosplayers a chance to get a little more original with their creations.

'Masquerades are still an important part of traditional science fiction conventions, both large and small,' says Miller. 'Since these conventions focus as much on the written literature as they do on comics or films – and possibly almost entirely so, depending on the convention – there is much more room for personal interpretation and invention. For instance, if an author merely describes his intergalactic hero as wearing "a uniform" or "space armour", the costumer can take that in any direction they like.'

Costumers as Luke Skywalker and Princess Leia from the *Star Wars* films, late 1970s.

A costumer at a convention in the 1970s.

I once saw a costumer who came dressed as an Orthodox Jew: black hat and coat, beard and ringlets, a loincloth and a sword. He was Cohen the Barbarian.

Costumers at a convention in the 1970s.

Schnaubelt (fourth from left) and friends as characters from the anime series
Space Pirate Captain Harlock.

Schnaubelt (far left) and friends as characters from the 1970s animated television
programme *Star Blazers.*

Karen Schnaubelt

COSPLAYER

'We were on the leading edge of the anime/cosplay wave,' says Karen Schnaubelt, a veteran of the American cosplay scene of the 1970s and '80s. 'People didn't always understand where the characters were from or what the costumes were, but we made them well enough that people liked them.'

Cosplaying as anime characters few had ever heard of (at the time, at least), Schnaubelt was living in a period when finding other people who shared your interests wasn't as easy as it is today. 'I had a pen pal in New York who I'd met through *Star Trek* fandom, and she would write me about trying to pull in episodes of *Captain Harlock* (in French!) by pointing her TV antenna out her apartment window in the Bronx and aiming it at Canada.'

Other ways America's first cosplay and anime nerds used to hang out was by belonging to sci-fi clubs and attending conventions. 'I remember a highlight of the 1978 World Science Fiction Convention was seeing episodes of *Astro Boy* that I had last seen first-run in 1964. And the 1983 convention did a late-night showing of *Arrivederci Yamato*, complete with live translator, which led to a funny moment where Captain Okita gave a five-minute inspirational speech on screen, and the English translation was: "Don't screw up".'

Fans could also get their anime fix and talk cosplay by meeting at the homes of people lucky enough to own a VCR. 'Anime was incredibly difficult to come by in the '70s and '80s. First, there was nothing available except broadcast TV until videotape became commonly available, and second, the import videotapes were heinously expensive – around $70 to $100 for a movie (or short collection of episodes). The cheapest blank videotapes were $18 each in those days, and videotape recorders were thousands of dollars to purchase. Each week, I would buy a blank tape for a friend of mine who had a VCR. He would record the episodes all week long, and then on Saturdays a group of us would gather at his apartment and watch a marathon of the episodes.'

Schnaubelt and her friends created their outfits with a level of quality and dedication to the source material that is impressive even by today's standards. Most people could appreciate their attention to detail – but not everybody: 'The only negative reaction we ever had was from the Ambassador Hotel in Los Angeles, when we hung our *Captain Harlock* and *Queen Emeraldas* pirate flags out our hotel window. The management asked us politely but pointedly to bring them back in, as they said it was giving the impression that the hotel had been taken over by terrorists!'

気分は、もうアニメヒーロー
「コスチューム・プレー」大作戦
Hero Costume Operation

♡クロードからラムちゃんまで、アニメ・ヒーロー、ヒロインのキャラを着こなす！コスチューム遊びはファン活動の究極。そのテクニックを徹底ルポ!!

カンペキ変身

ACT 1

燃えあがれ！ヒーロー！ヒーロー・パワー
君もコスチューム・プレーで人気ヒーロー

ブモモ…オレ幸せ！

コスプレ遊びの主な活動場所はコミック・マーケットなど同人誌即売会の会場。またファンクラブの集いや上映会などでも催しに花をそえる。特にコンテストがあったり、仮装パ

トラ宇宙人レイと……。マスクの中身がアニメと同じにしかしラン……!?

ーティーがあったりするワケじゃなく、とにかく目立ちたい騒ぎたい遊びゴコロなのだ。

もとはマーケットの参加者が自分たちの同人誌を売るために客引きやすいサンドイッチマンを兼ねて、思い思いのキャラクターに扮装していたもの。ところが最近では、同人誌とは独立して、会場では大勢力に。中には同人誌を売る側でなく、買う側にも、あてや

すかさず近寄ってご挨拶。カメラを持って行き、一緒に記念写真を撮るのも一案。また、自分と同じコスチュームの人がいた時には、そのアニメについての情報交換、お互いの同人誌の交換なんかも楽しいゾ！小道具やメカの出来

▶今回、登場願ったのはSFアクション・アニメ大好き少女の彩チャン。アニメ・ファンのサークル"Pi-ZZA"の会長さんをやっているんだって。演じるのは「未来警察ウラシマン」のクロードこと水沢蔵人。男役に挑戦だ。会場では、キャビキャビと、はしゃぎまくって自分たちの同人誌を売っているそうだ

→TV放映

Nobuyuki Takahashi's 'Hero Costume Operation' article in *My Anime* (June 1983).

Nobuyuki Takahashi

WRITER AND INNOVATOR

'Cosplay did not suddenly appear,' says Nobuyuki Takahashi. He should know: Takahashi helped popularise the term in the early 1980s.

In the 1970s, Japanese college students began dressing up as manga and anime characters. These young people had grown up on a steady diet of comics and cartoons, and when they attended manga and anime conventions (as well as school and university festivals), going in character was, as in the West, a way to express fandom.

Sci-fi conventions had existed in Japan since the 1960s, but in 1975 Comic Market (aka Comiket) launched, creating a venue for self-published comics. It was a fan convention and, in this environment, what would become cosplay in Japan started to flourish. There was already a Japanese term to express the concept of dressing up: *kasou* (仮想).

However, the word carried a nuance of disguise and didn't quite capture the spirit of what cosplay had become. In the West the word 'masquerade' could be used to refer to costuming, but when Takahashi and some university friends tried to translate 'masquerade' into Japanese for a magazine article they were writing, it sounded 'too noble and old fashioned'. According to Takahashi, 'We needed to find another way to express the concept.'

Various terms were floating around. 'We had heard the English word "costume" and seen events with names like "Costume Show", "Kasou Show", "Hero Play" and whanot,' says Takahashi. In Japanese, English and other foreign words are often combined and/or shortened, for brevity's sake. For example, the Japanese for 'remote control' – *rimooto kontorooru* – is shortened to *rimokon*. 'So we started to think of different combinations,' Takahashi says. 'Finally, we came up with "cosplay".' The term was a portmanteau of 'costume' and 'play'. It was perfect.

Takahashi's cosplay article appeared in the June 1983 issue of *My Anime*. It covered the fans who dressed up as manga and anime characters from the Comiket convention in Tokyo. The article featured an array of cosplayers in elaborate costumes: superheroes like Kamen Rider; realistic robot costumes from anime such as *Techno Police 21C*; anime heroes from *Lupin III* and *Star Blazers*; as well as sexy cosplay, like Lum Invader from *Urusei Yatsura*. There was even a special feature on female cosplayers who dress as male characters, something that continues to be popular today. Many of these types of characters – superheroes, robots and sexy characters – are still prevalent in both Japanese and international cosplay. Yet already in the early 1980s, cosplayers were excelling at them.

The *My Anime* article refers to both 'costume play' (コスチュームプレイ, *kosuchuumu purei*) and 'cosplay' (コスプレ, *kosupure*). Then there's the article's English title, 'Hero Costume Operation'. There's a reason for the discrepancy. According to Takahashi, 'When we were putting together that article, we were still in the process of thinking what we should call this activity. That's why it wasn't yet summed up in one word.' (Good thing 'hero costume operation' didn't catch on, huh?) While it's possible others in Japan also hit upon the term 'cosplay' at around the same time, this was the first time the word appeared in print.

At Japan's biggest comic book convention later that year, few people knew the term. According to Takahashi, a year or two later 'cosplay' was in wide use among fans attending manga and anime conventions. It wasn't until the '90s, though, after the subculture was introduced on television and in magazines, that the word finally hit a wider audience in Japan. Even Takahashi is surprised that, 30 years on, the term has caught on worldwide.

'Cosplay is a fan's expression of his or her love for a favourite character,' says Takahashi. 'Drawing a piece of artwork, writing a story, animating a movie and showing this to others is a manifestation of that love. And cosplay is one of those expressions in which fans use their entire bodies.' But has he ever cosplayed? 'Nope, not even once,' says Takahashi, who heads up a design and planning company for publishers and broadcasters. 'Typically, I wear casual clothes at the office. Whenever I wear a business suit, that's me cosplaying. It's a cosplay of a businessman.'

Above and facing: 'Hero Costume Operation' article in *My Anime* (June 1983).

Hero Costume Operation

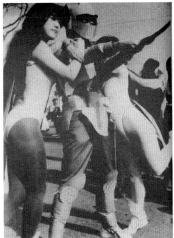

◆全員集合した「ダンバイン」登場キャラ。どのグループも、根むと気軽に写真用のポーズをとってくれるのです

◆出た！ 通常ユニフォームとバトル・プロテクターニ人のウランマリュウ。左の男の子はトレーナーを利用しているとか

◆ウワッ！ スピンナー・スチックを手にするモモがカワイイ。この他、男の子の女装モモも（ウェ）

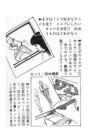

◆まずはＴＶで好きなアニメを見てコスプレしたいキャラを決定！！ 仮合うものなどはどれかな？

カット／田中横見

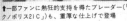

▲一部ファンに熱狂的支持を得たブレーダー（「テクノポリス21Ｃ」）も、重厚な仕上げで登場

出番が少ないからコミケに登場

◆こちらボール紙、プラスチック製のオーラバトラー！ 羽根や角の鋭さがカッコイイ

How to build Mecha Suite

　上手なメカ スーツを作るには とにかく模型製作の心得がなくちゃダメ。そして必ず図面を描くこと。できれば簡単なダミーを作るといい。気をつけるのは関節部分の作りと どうすれば体にフィットできるかの工夫。これをシッカリ考えておかないと体のまわりでメカがグラグラする。素材の大半は重さの関係もあって段ボールなど紙を使おう。

♥コスプレPHOTO大募集！！

素材探しがポイント！ コスプレ・メーキング・ガイド

マテリアル・ショップ

◎素材探しのポイントは コスプレに使えそうな材料が置いてある店を広範囲に知っておくこと。服を作るのだからして 生地や和洋裁材料店には必ず足を運ぶこと。ボタン ファスナー リボンなど応用できるものは数多い。レオタードは専門のスポーツウェアショップだが チャコット（東京 渋谷☎476-1311 などでは幅広くタイプを揃え通販も行っている。

　模型材料店 日曜大工専門店 画材店なども見逃せない。メカ物や小道具を作る時に必要なプラスチック 合成樹脂の布など それに便利な工具類もたくさんある。東急ハンズ（東京 渋谷☎476-5461）のように１カ所で全部がそろう店もあるゾ

☆自分

Inside a Cospa shop in the Akihabara area of Tokyo.

Accessories on sale include wigs and fake samurai swords.

Cosplay World

Yoshiyuki Matsunaga

ENTREPRENEUR

In Japan in the 1990s, if you liked anime, music, wearing costumes and soaking up geek culture, 'cosplay dance parties' were the thing to attend. 'The costume dance parties were featured on television and in magazines,' recalls Yoshiyuki Matsunaga. While the parties – often held at the coolest Tokyo bars and clubs – were a big hit, not all attendees were as good with a needle and thread as they were on the dance floor.

'In May 1995 we opened a cosplay store in Shibuya,' Matsunaga says. Called Cospa, it aimed to sell quality costumes to clubbers as well as those attending conventions like Comiket. Today, the company is synonymous with high-quality cosplay outfits, which it sells in retail spaces across Japan. 'When we opened the shop for the first time, I had no idea whether or not customers would come. I was blown away when we opened the doors and there were a hundred people in line. I felt so thankful that people just came, because we really didn't have that many things for sale yet.'

Having people lined up around the block was a pretty big achievement for someone who was himself relatively new to the world of cosplay. 'I had first heard the word "cosplay" in 1993,' says Matsunaga. 'It was differentiated from *kasou*, the Japanese word for "masquerade". Even "costume play" was originally used in the sex industry in Japan,

but after the word entered wider use, that association was no longer made.'

Cospa was instrumental in helping to change the image of cosplay in Japan. For example, locating the store in Shibuya, Tokyo's youth fashion centre, instead of Akihabara, the city's technology and anime geek district, shows that Cospa's founders immediately saw the connection between cosplay and fashion. Prior to Cospa, fans would have sold home-made costumes at conventions. Working directly with anime, manga and game companies, Cospa now makes quality ready-made costumes that are not just available in Japan but sold worldwide. It also enables those who aren't necessarily DIY types to enjoy cosplay.

A cosplay retail shop might be good business, then, but it also democratises the scene by making high-quality costumes available to all. The excuse of not being able to sew no longer stands up. 'At Cospa, we want to support those who want to cosplay but don't make their own costumes, as well as cosplayers who do make their own outfits, by offering, for example, costume accessories like buttons or badges worn by their favourite characters to make their outfits more accurate,' says Matsunaga. 'Basically, we are always thinking about what we can do for those who love cosplay.'

Yoshiyuki Matsunaga

Giorgia as Maleficent from Disney's animated film *Sleeping Beauty*.

Giorgia

COSPLAYER

The fact that she has watched Japanese cartoons since she was a kid makes it hard for Giorgia to pinpoint when exactly she fell in love with them, though she does remember that, during the early 1990s, Italians began to take more intérest in anime and manga. In the mid-1990s, she was attending Lucca Comics & Games, the most important comic convention in Italy. 'I saw a few guys wearing fantasy costumes of ogres, wizards and knights, and a few others wearing costumes from *Star Trek*,' she says. 'I said to myself: "If they can do that with their favourite characters, why can't I do the same with mine?"'

The next year, when she returned to the same convention, Giorgia and some friends decided to go in costume. She dressed as Sailor Mars from the Japanese series *Sailor Moon*. 'At that time we didn't know we were cosplaying and we just called it "wearing costumes",' she recalls. 'It was only later, on the verge of the new century – when I had Internet access – that I came to know that this kind of hobby had a name and existed worldwide, so I guess that cosplay and I met halfway.'

In the late 1970s Italy experienced an anime invasion, with Japanese cartoons being broadcast on local TV. The anime was often re-coloured, edited and featured terrible dubbing. Nevertheless, young Giorgia grew up watching classic anime series like *Heidi, Girl of the Alps* (directed by Studio Ghibli co-founder Isao Takahata) and *UFO Robot Grendizer*, the Super Robot anime series created by Go Nagai.

However, getting access to particular anime that weren't shown on Italian TV was tricky. 'All that we could share were VHS tapes with old and barely visible recordings, made by someone who had one of the first video recorders and copied on from fan to fan,' she remembers. 'I started cosplaying in a time when we anime fans had to fight for the littlest scrap of paper with a picture of our heroes on it.'

Giorgia didn't think her hobby was ever going to be taken seriously, let alone spread like it has. 'A very close friend of mine always says that our example made younger generations realise that bringing our heroes alive was possible, contributing to the cosplay boom. I don't know if this is true, but if it is, I'm glad I've been part of it.'

Giorgia as Litchi Faye-Ling from the video game series *BlazBlue*.

Giorgia as Black Widow from Marvel Comics.

Kamui

OSPLAYER

hen Svetlana 'Kamui' Quindt graduated from
iversity, she could have gone and got a 'real'
o. Instead, she has ended up making a living
rough cosplay, writing her own books on costume
nstruction. 'These days it's become very easy
get into cosplay since you can find tutorials for
most everything,' she explains.

When Kamui started cosplaying over ten years
go, things weren't so simple. Perhaps one of the
ggest barriers was a reluctance to share openly:
ck then, according to Kamui, many cosplayers
dn't talk about the materials they used or their
stume making techniques. 'They preferred to keep
eir process a secret,' she says, 'maybe because they
re scared that other cosplayers would steal their
eas or methods.' Today, it's a different world. Social
edia has changed the way people can share and
scuss their work, a move Kamui thinks was for the
st. 'Followers and fans encourage cosplayers now
document progress stories of every costume, and
also become very common to create tutorials

support other cosplayers and help newcomers get
into this wonderful hobby,' says Kamui. 'The cosplay
community is now one huge network . . . connected
from every part of the world.'

Kamui's experience also means she's well
placed to offer advice to those looking to start
building their own outfits. 'You are able to learn
everything you need without spending much time
or money,' she says. 'You don't need to experiment,
either, nor fail and waste expensive materials. You
can just watch and learn, take your time and do your
homework. You don't need to be rich, you don't need
to be a student with too much time on your hands
and you also don't need to have wicked prop making
skills. All you need is your will to create something.'

Kamui as Wonder Woman.

Kamui as a Protoss Wizard from the video game series *StarCraft*.

Kamui as a druid from the video game *World of Warcraft*.

Kamui as Alexstrasza the Life-Binder from the video game series *Diablo*.

Kamui as a gladiator from the video game *Aion: The Tower of Eternity*.

Gibson as Toko from the video game *Super Galdelic Hour*.

Omi Gibson

COSPLAYER

'I'm really shy,' confesses Omi Gibson. You wouldn't know it from her edgy and often sexy cosplay, which shows she's just as comfortable playing the seductress as she is the psychotic villain.

Gibson, who now models in her native Tokyo, began cosplaying as a little girl, way before she had any idea what cosplay actually was. She was seven or eight years old and smitten with the 1985 Hong Kong horror spoof *Mr Vampire*. She decided to dress up like the movie's *jiangshi* – hopping vampires or zombies from Chinese folklore. 'I think my parents thought I was a pretty strange kid,' she recalls. But that doesn't mean there was resistance against her developing hobby – in fact, 'Now my mum totally wants to try cosplay . . . When a T-shirt featuring my cosplay went on sale, mum was totally jealous.'

It wasn't until she was thirteen or fourteen that Gibson first attended an event in full cosplay regalia. At a con sponsored by the Japanese gaming magazine *Famitsu*, she dressed as Gillian Seed, the hard-boiled detective from the *Blade Runner-*inspired game *Snatcher*. Since then, she's been able to switch smoothly between dressing as femmes fatales and as macho males. Gibson often engages in 'crossplay', which is when a cosplayer dresses as someone of a different gender. (A similar twist is 'gender-bending' cosplay, in which a cosplayer flips a character's gender to match their own, modifying the character's appearance and costume along the way.)

Gibson originally worked as an assistant to manga artist Tsukasa Kotobuki, honing her drawing skills and developing a good eye for style and presentation, as well as a strong work ethic. 'It was tough being a manga assistant,' she recalls. 'You wouldn't sleep for two or three days right before the publishing deadline.' She's since traded drawing characters with pencil and paper for bringing them to life with fabric and photos: 'What's appealing about cosplay is that I can show a side of myself that I don't usually.'

Gibson as Cyborg Ninja from the *Metal Gear Solid* series.

Gibson as a Militaires sans Frontières soldier from the *Metal Gear Solid* series.

Gibson as Raiden from the *Metal Gear Solid* series.

Gibson as The Boss from the *Metal Gear Solid* series.

Kyle Johnsen

WEBSITE OWNER AND PHOTOGRAPHER

Cosplay.com was created with one goal in mind: to give all cosplayers, no matter where they were in the world, a single place to hang out. Before the site launched in 2002, there was no such thing as an online cosplay community. Instead, individual cosplayers congregated on sites like LiveJournal or via mailing lists.

'Back in 2002 I was running a business trying to publish a role-playing game system, and I also ran a popular online role-playing game community,' says Kyle Johnsen, Cosplay.com's owner and founder. 'My girlfriend at the time was really into cosplay, so I pulled from my community experience and started Cosplay.com to have something to do while we were attending conventions together.' Johnsen had no idea how quickly it would take off. By the end of the year, he was working on it full-time. Cosplay.com has since emerged as one of the culture's largest online homes, alongside the artwork-sharing network DeviantArt.

As big an influence dedicated websites like Cosplay.com have had on cosplay, however, social media services such as Twitter and Facebook have helped shape the community even more dramatically, sometimes with mixed results. 'Social media has accomplished two things in the cosplay realm: it has given cosplayers the perfect opportunity to promote themselves to a larger audience, and it has also fragmented the community again somewhat,' Johnsen explains. 'Ten years ago, to be well-known in cosplay you had to really work at it, creating great costumes and attending a lot of conventions. Now you can practically do the same thing overnight with a good photo shoot and a social media plan.'

In the past, most prominent cosplayers knew each other. That's no longer true. 'Now,' Johnsen says, 'you see someone announced as a guest signing autographs at an event and sometimes find yourself saying, "Who?" Then you look them up and see that they already have 50,000 fans on Facebook. I'm not saying that it's a good or a bad thing, but social media has definitely reshaped the playing field.'

In addition to his work with the website, Johnsen has also spent much of the last decade as a member of the community himself, as a photographer of cosplay, taking pictures all over the globe. 'I was very active with cosplay photography for many years, covering conventions and putting galleries up on the website, as well as doing feature shoots for *Cosmode* magazine,' he says. 'Nowadays, I mostly do a photo shoot here or there of something I'm really into and feel I can have some artistic licence with.'

Vitaliya Abramova, original creation.

I think that there is a general misconception that cosplayers are attention-seeking by nature. Personally, I think cosplay is just a natural outlet for the innate human desire to be socially engaged and recognised for something. It just happens to also be combined with something creative and awesome.

Jia Jem as Tank Girl.

Wigs are always difficult. A lot of characters have hairstyles that would be impossible to translate to your real hair. That's why I love wigs so much! They're not hair, and you can do a lot of funky stuff with them! They come in a wonderful wide range of awesome colours and blends . . . it used to not be that way.

HezaChan

COSPLAYER

'I figured if people dressed up at *Star Trek* conventions, then they probably did it at anime conventions as well,' says HezaChan. Once she'd started, she was thrilled to find others who cosplayed and began making friends in the scene.

HezaChan finds her inspiration in anime and video game characters she feels she can relate to and that stand out visually. 'I then get this huge urge to make their costume,' she says. 'I'll keep drawing that character to hype myself up for the construction of the costume.' At first HezaChan got a little help from her mother with the sewing, but she soon cut loose and learned how to make her own costumes: 'I just winged it . . . there was a lot of trial and error.' But does cosplay still allow room for mistakes?

'As someone who never really fit in, I found that cosplay and cons in the early 2000s were much more relaxed, with people who seemed to be much more inviting and friendly.' People worked hard on their costumes, she explains, but there wasn't as huge a concern with accuracy as there is today. Nobody seemed to care if your eye colour was off. 'It seems like people weren't as judgmental as they are now, which is quite sad. For a new, younger person – especially girls – trying to get into cosplay now, it must be a bit scary,' she says. 'You see all these negative comments on the Internet calling people fat, ugly, or just ripping apart their costume.'

New cosplayers shouldn't be discouraged by the Internet, though – not everyone's a jerk, and it provides a place to pick up tips and connect with others in a positive way. 'All the blood, sweat and tears are totally worth it when others appreciate your work, and you can bond over the love of the character or series you're cosplaying from.'

Yaya Han

COSPLAYER

In the 1990s, Yaya Han was living in Arizona and had joined her first anime club. 'Everyone talked about Anime Expo like the mecca for anime fans, and the club actually organised a bus trip to LA for the convention,' says Han. 'I was told that some people dressed up as anime characters at the event, and some part of me wanted to do it, too.'

Soon, she was doing just that. These days, it's what Han does for a living. Her first attempt at cosplay was, she recalls, 'very bad'. But she has never forgotten the pride she felt in sewing the outfit herself, in making something from scratch, and the feeling she got when someone asked her for a photo. 'I strongly believe that cosplay is so magnetic to me because of both the craftsmanship side and the performance aspect,' she says. 'Without either, I wouldn't enjoy it as much.'

While growing up in China and Germany, Han was always reading manga, watching anime and drawing, drawing, drawing. For her, putting pen to paper was a way to express her love for a certain character. Later, she would discover a way to do that, and more, by transforming into the character. 'Once I discovered cosplay, that artistic streak and my anime

Han as Carmilla from the anime film
Vampire Hunter D: Bloodlust.

Han as Fiora Laurent from the video game *League of Legends*.

fandom naturally transferred to making costumes,' she explains. 'I could become those characters I loved through cosplaying them, and the artist in me got to learn a whole world of new things.'

Each costume brings a new challenge. In the early days, she picked characters she adored and costumes she felt she was able to make. But with each passing outfit, Han's craft improved and her range got bigger: she has now cosplayed as over 250 characters. Her cosplay creations have been through many phases, from winged costumes to dresses with giant ruffles to highly elaborate, corsetted get-ups.

'These days cosplay is more than just my hobby, it is my business,' says Han, who now cosplays professionally, appearing at conventions around the world. 'I have to consider things such as transportability to overseas conventions, weather and heat.' Crucially, outfits must be comfortable enough for her to spend the day in, whether she's posing for photos, judging costume competitions or giving talks on the subject.

Han is one of the first cosplayers to successfully turn their hobby into a full-time job. She still makes all her own costumes, and works as hard as she can on putting out consistently high-quality cosplay. 'While I benefit from cosplay becoming an industry, I try very hard to stay true to what got me into cosplay all those years ago,' she says. 'Where cosplay will go, I don't know, but I will keep on trucking, cosplaying my way.'

Han as a Dark Elf from the online role-playing game *Lineage*.

As I get older I have been embracing my plus-size body and making costumes more 'suited' to my body type. Not because I feel that I have to or because some person thinks I should only cosplay 'my body type', but because I want to celebrate these awesome chubby ladies, or men, and give them the fan love they deserve.

Thea Teufel

COSPLAYER

'When I started cosplaying at anime conventions it was a much smaller crowd,' says Thea Teufel, who has been cosplaying since the 1990s. 'Most people seemed to make one costume for the whole year and wear it to all the local conventions. Nobody seemed to care if you had a wig or used your natural hair. You never really heard people make rude comments if your costume wasn't 100 per cent accurate.'

As cosplay became more popular and moved online in the early 2000s, however, Teufel began to notice a change: 'Very quickly, cosplay became more of a popularity contest.' According to Teufel, some of the individuals just coming into cosplay at the time were more concerned with becoming a 'popular'

cosplayer than simply perfecting their outfits and enjoying the hobby. The Internet also provided a space for those who were more than happy to write offensive, disparaging comments about others.

This isn't to say that she has become disillusioned with cosplay, however – far from it. Despite the many problems the Internet has created for the cosplay scene, it has also allowed Teufel to make new friends and rediscover her love of the culture. 'Lately I've met lots of young, new cosplayers who are accepting of all people, open-minded, and who just love the craft of cosplay. They have renewed my passion for the hobby.'

Checkley as Savage Opress from the animated series *Star Wars: The Clone Wars*.

Julian Checkley

COSPLAYER

'I've been cosplaying almost all my life, ever since I made my first Darth Vader costume at the age of seven,' says British cosplayer Julian Checkley. 'It was one of those papier mâché jobs plastered onto a balloon, and I had to steal my grandfather's sunglasses so I could pop the lenses out and glue them on to complete the helmet eyepieces.'

This boyhood love of papier mâché developed, and Checkley decided to pursue an education and a career in making costumes. But he may have thought he'd made a mistake when he found himself studying hair and make-up alongside fashion industry hopefuls in London. A job in TV creating monster suits and special effects would soon follow, however, where he would not just learn how to develop visual effects and make fantastical creatures, but gain experience performing inside them as well. 'One of the first costumes I put together was Darth Maul,' says Checkley. In preparation, he did loads of research, finding the right fabrics, sculpting horns and even locating the same type of boots the actor wore. 'But when I eventually suited up and went to my first event, I stuck out like a sore thumb. Being 6 foot 6, I towered above the resident Vader and other troopers. It just looked wrong.'

Checkley and his wife later moved to Ireland, leaving the TV business behind to sell luxury perfume. He now has time to hit the gym each week to maintain his physique, and spends probably a lot more than the average cosplayer on his craft, in terms of both time and money. 'Because this is my sole hobby and passion, my budget for doing it is set pretty high,' he says. 'This also allows me to take the costumes to the next level, not only in creating the look of the character but making them . . . function in reality. Every piece of the costume is sculpted, fabricated, painted and weathered as accurately as possible. These costumes don't just have to look good, but also perform well and be resilient when I put the suit on.'

The results speak for themselves. Yet despite all the effort Checkley puts into his cosplay, and all the incredible costumes he's made so far, there is one outfit that still eludes him: 'To give you an example of the extremes of money that gets spent, the only time I have backed away from a costume was when I priced up building a costume of Lord Sauron from *The Lord of the Rings*. To make that costume to the standard I wanted, I was looking at a price in excess of £12,000 [$20,000]. Who knows? Maybe one day.'

Checkley as Tarfful from *Star Wars*.

A young Checkley as Darth Vader.

The adult Checkley as Darth Vader.

Julian Checkley

Merritt as April O'Neil from the animated series *Teenage Mutant Ninja Turtles.*

Lindze Merritt

COSPLAYER

Lindze Merritt discovered cosplay by accident while researching a Halloween costume back in 1999. 'I've always had a love for making things, dressing up, and general costume love,' she explains, 'so I was thrilled to find a whole scene revolving around those ideas.' Merritt now works at a photography studio, alongside photographer and friend Allison Rose, as a make-up and hair stylist.

'I started doing make-up primarily for cosplayers and friends, and when I realised I loved it, I took classes to learn more about the profession,' she says. 'Cosplay was definitely the gateway, for both me and Allison, to our current career paths, since we're both cosplayers.'

Merritt's work life and personal life come together at major conventions, where she often takes make-up commissions to help other cosplayers bring their characters to life. 'Recently, I opened up my schedule for make-up and booked around ten jobs for a convention weekend. It was really fun because doing cosplay make-up is more adventurous and interesting than my usual make-up jobs.'

Merritt as Miranda Lawson from the video game series *Mass Effect*.

Goldy

COSPLAYER AND COSPLAY TEACHER

Once a month, in Tokyo's geek district of Akihabara, students sit down for lessons. But in Goldy's classroom, they don't learn about science, maths or literature. They get a masterclass in cosplay.

For over a decade, Goldy has been a regular on the Japanese cosplay circuit, appearing at manga and anime events as robots and giant mecha. 'I love robots,' he laughs. 'Probably because I'm a dude.' Japan has a long-standing romance with mechanised characters. 'In the past, robot characters like Astro Boy and Gigantor gave many Japanese kids dreams of the future,' he says. 'Then, *Mazinger Z* and *Gundam* and more recently *Macross* and *Neon Genesis Evangelion* have done the same by evolving and meeting the needs of each successive generation – which is why I think robot and mecha-style characters have remained popular for so long in Japan.'

After graduating from university, Goldy moved from his native Japan to the United States to study English. 'I remember how much I enjoyed Halloween when I lived in the US.' Goldy now spends his free time making enormous and elaborate polyurethane suits, which can take up to four months to complete. The most difficult costumes to make have curved surfaces, so *Evangelion* suits are harder to make than *Gundam* ones.

Goldy's monthly cosplay class teaches the fine art of constructing complex robot gear in wearable polyurethane, and is open to everyone – he encourages foreigners to sign up via the English-language page on his website. 'To be honest, the real reason I do the class is to provide foreigners visiting Japan with a new style of cultural exchange,' he says. 'I'd like the class to be a place for foreigners who come to Akihabara but don't know where they can meet Japanese people with similar interests.' Goldy continues: 'For me, cosplay is appealing in that it surpasses the differences in language by offering a path to mutual understanding.'

Ed Hoff

COSPLAYER AND ACADEMIC

Ed Hoff, a Canadian cosplayer, has lived in Japan since 1998. He is currently studying for a PhD on the globalisation of cosplay at Nagoya University and is also involved with the annual World Cosplay Summit. So when it comes to cosplay, you can't get much more connected than this. But it wasn't always that way.

'It can be a little tough to make friends in the community,' Hoff explains. 'If you go out to an event in Japan and just start introducing yourself, people will look at you weird.' Instead, he says, you usually first start by meeting a friend of a friend. You can exchange cosplay cards (essentially business cards for cosplayers) and then stay in touch via a cosplay social networking site such as Cure. 'This can grow into a friendship after further meetings at other cosplay events. The way you go about meeting new people through cosplay [in Japan] is less forward than you would find in other countries.'

Hoff grew up in a suburb of Vancouver. While his youth was spent watching Japanese cartoons like *Star Blazers* and *Robotech* and playing video games, he didn't know how pervasive *otaku* ('geek') culture was in Japan before he arrived. 'Advertising for anime and manga is really everywhere ... in convenience stores, on train station advertisement boards and on TV.' Around the turn of this century Hoff was living in Nagoya where, after a chance meeting, he made some friends who worked at a local television station. That station was Aichi TV, which would later go on to create the World Cosplay Summit (WCS), now one of the biggest international cosplay events.

While cosplay events in Japan tend to be fairly formal, the WCS is trying to break down barriers, especially the ones that exist between cosplayers and wider society. As Hoff explains, cosplayers in Japan tend to appear only in 'safe' areas such as at conventions, as they worry that walking around in costume among the general public might upset or annoy non-cosplayers. 'With the WCS, we try to promote a weekend where it's alright to walk around downtown in costume,' says Hoff. 'Informing businesses of this standard and petitioning their support through offering deals for people who come to their store in costume are ways to show cosplayers and non-cosplayers alike that cosplay is something that everyone can enjoy, and it doesn't need to be hidden away.'

Hoff as Evangelion Unit-00 and other characters from the animated series *Neon Genesis Evangelion*.

Danny Kelley as Superman.

Andrew Michael Phillips

PHOTOGRAPHER

Cosplay and high fashion may seem strange bedfellows, but where fashion and portrait photographer Andrew Michael Phillips is concerned, the two worlds aren't far apart. Amazed by the outfits worn by cosplayers but disappointed by the presentation of existing cosplay shots, Phillips got into photographing the culture himself. 'The thing that kept bugging me was that most of the photos were ruined by the convention floor or surrounding environment. While it's interesting seeing cosplayers in their element, which is on the convention floor, I knew that I could better show the incredible amount of work and detail in the costumes by using the same tools I utilise for my high-fashion photography.'

Much of Phillips's cosplay work brings his subject into the studio, where he can capture their outfit and performance in a controlled setting.

'It is very similar to my fashion work because it is handmade garments worn by an amazing model,' he says. 'In both instances I am also trying to capture the garments or costume in a flattering light. I go more "dramatic" in situations that call for it, and I go for "beauty" for others.'

It's not only lighting and camera tricks that carry over from his fashion photography skill set; he also brings in a team of professionals from the fashion world. 'Hair and make-up experts are there for the models, and I work with a designer on occasion when I need backgrounds that are beyond my skills.'

As a comics fan, it's a cosplayer's ability to interpret and personify fiction that Phillips likes most. 'I enjoy the energy each cosplayer brings,' he explains. 'They literally embody the character and bring the comic to life.'

Margie Cox as She-Hulk.

Jonathan Carroll as the Wolverine from *X-Men*.

Andrew Michael Phillips

Chaka Cumberbatch

COSPLAYER

Growing up, Chaka Cumberbatch lived in a very strict Christian household, where Halloween – a favourite holiday of hers – wasn't celebrated. So it was through the theatre that she got a chance to not only act but also dress up in a variety of costumes. 'Telling your costume-obsessed child that she's not allowed to dress up on Halloween is basically paving the way for a lifelong fascination with costuming,' she says. 'When you take a love for costumes and mix it with a love for comics and cartoons, cosplay is the next logical step.'

With a father in the US Air Force, Cumberbatch spent her childhood in Okinawa, Japan. She was fascinated by the country's manga and anime, and they would later become major inspirations. In high school, back in the United States, her interests turned to American comics. Cosplay soon followed. 'I pick my characters based on my passion first, and difficulty level second,' says Cumberbatch, who works at an anime distributor and as a freelance writer. 'Cosplay is too costly, too time-consuming and labour-intensive to spend on a character you don't love, so I only pick characters I'm crazy about.'

Whether from the DC Comics universe or *Sailor Moon*, Cumberbatch lets her love of specific characters lead her choices. 'Some people like to use "accuracy" as an excuse to impose rules on what people are "allowed" to cosplay, based on what they look like, but honestly, I don't see why most comic book or video game cosplay can't be for everyone,' she says. 'If you can pick up a comic book or pick up a controller and fall in love with a character, you're allowed to make a costume and pay them homage. Your race, age, size or body shape shouldn't matter. I honestly think that some people look at a character and see that character's race as the most defining characteristic,' she states. 'Would Wonder Woman be any less powerful if she wasn't white? Would it matter if Batman was black under his mask?'

'Cosplay is short for "costume play",' Cumberbatch continues. 'Race is not a costume. It's not something you can put on or take off for play. So why does it matter? It should be beside the point.'

Cumberbatch as Akasha from the film *Queen of the Damned*.

Cumberbatch as Bulma from the anime series *Dragon Ball Z*.

Thorsson as a Spartan from the video game series *Halo*.

Shawn Thorsson

COSPLAYER AND MAKER

Shawn Thorsson recalls how he excited he was, after being stationed in Japan for a couple of years with the US Navy, to be back home for a 'proper' Halloween. He loved *Star Wars* as a kid, so he decided to go as a Stormtrooper for the night. 'Looking around, I wasn't able to find any makers that offered armour in my size, so I thought, "If they can figure out how to make it, there's no reason I can't figure it out, too."'

Thorsson did figure it out – and it would change his life forever. 'The next year, I started getting ready for Halloween in March and just barely managed to get a passable suit of armour together in time.' The project took more time, money and energy than he could ever have imagined, but it didn't matter. He was hooked.

Thorsson has since left the Navy to work exclusively in his workshop, where he builds replica weapons and armour as well as a line of militarised garden gnomes. And though he's constantly creating commissioned work for individuals and companies,

it's his personal projects that end up getting the most attention. 'I like to make things. There's always tonnes of tiny little challenges along the way. It's a constant puzzle-solving exercise with countless moving parts and a tremendous variety of ways to approach each new part. I learn something new with every project.' Even though he's not much of a gamer, Thorsson has made plenty of video game outfits and accessories. 'If I see a character design that I find particularly interesting. I'll often find myself wearing an exact replica from head to toe long before I actually find the time to sit down and play the game that it comes from.'

The process itself is engaging, but the final results are stunning. Thorsson says he gets the most satisfaction from people's reactions to his work. 'In the end, as much as I love the finished pieces, they're really nothing compared to the big grin on some kid's face when I turn the corner and he finds himself face-to-face with something he thought existed only in movies or video games.'

Thorsson and friends as various characters from series
including *Halo*, *Warhammer*, *Predator* and *Dead Space*.

Alodia Gosiengfiao

COSPLAYER

Alodia Gosiengfiao is a star. She has hundreds of thousands of Twitter followers, numerous product endorsement deals with international companies, a record deal and makes TV and movie appearances – and, let's not forget, does some wonderful cosplay as well.

'Believe or not,' says Gosiengfiao, 'my greatest fear when growing up was public speaking, so I really couldn't talk in front of my class and I always hid whenever someone brought out a camera. But cosplay has helped me overcome this fear.' Propelled by her love of the game *Ragnarok Online*, Gosiengfiao began cosplaying when she was fifteen years old in her native Philippines. She found she was pretty good at it, too, winning awards at local competitions. By the time she had graduated from university, she was already making international live appearances and garnering attention both online and in print.

Gosiengfiao loves making her own props, whether they're weapons, body armour or wigs. Cosplay is a way for her to combine her love of fashion, art, video games and anime – and to work up the courage to share that love with others. 'I like trying out different personas . . . I've done sweet characters, evil characters, monsters, angels, fairies, even mermaids.'

As well as the multitude of artistic and crafting skills she's developed, over the years she has learned how to perform for an audience – both of which are incredibly important in cosplay. But now that she's mastered the fantasy world of cosplay, she's keen to do the same for mundane daily tasks: 'I think I'd love to learn a few more essentials in life, like driving . . . driving in Manila is terrifying, but let's see!'

Gosiengfiao as Morrigan Aensland from the video game series *Darkstalkers*.

Alodia Gosiengfiao

Boer as Naked Snake from the *Metal Gear* video game series.

I cosplay to recreate an image of a character in real life. It's like drawing or painting, but on so many levels it is much more challenging than that.

Rick Boer

COSPLAYER

'At a certain age I just had to accept the fact that I was too old to play with my *Star Wars* figures,' says Rick Boer. 'So I recreated my favourite one – Boba Fett – in real life.'

Since then, Boer, also a big video game fan, has gone on to focus on bringing the characters he loves from the digital world into the real one. However, trying to copy a virtual outfit using actual materials can cause headaches. 'Capes, armour and sturdy leather items all warp and stretch to different sizes in games. In real life, things don't work that way,' says Boer. 'The challenge is to make the costume look exactly like what you see in-game. It involves a lot of cheating and hiding of different attachments and materials but it's fun to do.'

Not that he'd have it any other way. Should game developers pay more attention to how real-life materials work? 'No way. It wouldn't benefit the game experience in most cases, and game characters would probably end up looking a lot less cool. I mean . . . take *Assassin's Creed*. Wearing a hood that diminishes your sight to just about nothing when dashing across rooftops and scaling large structures wouldn't be very helpful and just isn't realistic. But it looks cool.'

Boer as Naked Snake from the *Metal Gear* video game series.

Boer as Naked Snake from the *Metal Gear* games.

Nebulaluben as Lilith and Roland from the *Borderlands* video games.

Nebulaluben

Laura Sánchez and her boyfriend Erik Guzmán began cosplaying together in 2008 as Nebulaluben, though it was a calling that had been years in the making. 'When I was a teenager, my granny bought me a sewing machine,' Sánchez says. 'At that time I used to go to funky dance classes and I wanted to make my own clothes for our dance festivals.' She loved taking apart old clothes to see how they were constructed. She admits, however, that her own original creations were 'nothing special'. But in 2008, after finishing her studies, Sánchez suddenly found herself with a lot of free time. She also went through a period of battling depression. 'I started having an anxiety crisis. A psychologist recommended I take up an absorbing hobby to forget about my problems, and focus on something creative.'

Cosplay seemed an ideal fit, and her boyfriend needed little convincing to join in. 'I've always loved martial arts and *sentai* ['task force'] series,' says Guzmán. 'During my childhood, I was living in Ecuador and those series were very popular. I loved their fighting choreography and I tried to imitate them, making my own weapons at home.'

Growing up, it seemed like Guzmán's house was always under construction. The upper floor was filled with tools, which he would use to build his own toy weapons. 'My father really enjoyed DIY and he used to take me with him every time he fixed something at home,' says Guzmán. 'He's always been very creative, a real craft enthusiast, so I could say he was – and still is – a big inspiration and support for me.'

But it wasn't until he moved to Spain that Guzmán discovered cosplay and prop making. 'Right after arriving in Spain, I also met Laura and started hanging out with her,' he says. 'Years later, we attended our first convention and thought we could make our own costumes. We joined our creative skills and curiosity to construct them, and we enjoyed the process and the result so much that we have kept on making costumes.' It was a decision that would change both of their lives, but Sánchez's especially. 'I can affirm that cosplaying saved me from depression. I found a creative activity that makes me keep on learning, makes me feel useful and that makes me able to express my gaming passion. I'll never be grateful enough for this hobby!'

Guzmán as Zer0 from the *Borderlands* video games.

Allegriana

COSPLAYER

For most characters, getting the cosplay right involves a specific dress, the perfect accessory, or maybe a colourful wig. When it comes to others, though, the costume doesn't stop at the sleeves: it covers the skin in outrageous or unnatural hues. For this, body paint, a substance Allegriana knows well, is used. 'I'm a huge *Star Wars* fan,' she says. 'I don't remember how I first came across the character Darth Talon. I think I saw some artwork of her and I was really intrigued; she's very visually striking.'

To become Darth Talon, Allegriana needs to be covered entirely in paint, which takes a long time and is 'a miserable process – I'm on my feet for hours and have to stand very still'. On top of that, there's the early start time needed for Allegriana's cosplay to be completed in time for whichever convention she is attending that day. To bring the character to life, Allegriana's sister Lyssa, an art student, handles the painting. An alcohol-based airbrush paint is used to colour the body, while a gentler water-based paint is used for the face. 'I honestly forget that I'm wearing it, so it's quite comfortable, and your skin can breathe just fine,' says Allegriana. 'But it is very difficult to get the alcohol-based paint off!' Unfortunately, for that, she has to pretty much shower in rubbing alcohol and 'scrub like crazy'.

Allegriana, who is also known as the 'Chainmail Chick' online for her love of medieval mail, says that people who don't cosplay can't understand the way that 'as soon as you put on that costume and step out of your room, you're a whole different person. People address you and treat you like your character, they want your picture, they want to play along with you. It's this wonderful give-and-take where you get to create that "Oh wow!" moment for other people, and they make you feel like all the hard work was absolutely worth it with their reactions.'

Crabcat Industries

COSPLAYERS AND BUSINESS OWNERS

'I was five years old, strapped a pillow to my back and said I was a Koopa Troopa from *Super Mario Bros*', says Holly Conrad of her first experience with what would become a lifelong passion. 'Cosplaying is something that I've always loved, even when I was a little kid and had no idea what I was doing.'

Conrad and her business partner Jessica Merizan run Crabcat Industries, a company that not only makes costumes for cosplayers and collectors but works with the entertainment industry on commercials and events. They've become a full-fledged special effects house and creature workshop, and Conrad has even hosted a TV show on cosplay – no wonder film-maker Guillermo del Toro hired Crabcat Industries to make a monster for a *Pacific Rim* promotional video.

'Bringing characters to life is something really special, and really fun,' Conrad says. 'Seeing someone get excited about your cosplay on the floor and really bond with you over a character you both love is why I keep doing it, and why I always try to get better and better. That's really what Crabcat is about: getting better at your craft with friends and being a supportive community for cosplay and anything else you do.'

The pair have been cosplaying together since 2007 and, as you might expect, they take their hobby seriously, with Merizan even managing to cover cosplay in her university studies. 'I've always loved performing and theatre. Cosplay is just another way for me to get on stage and express myself,' she says. 'I actually did my dissertation on the subject of cosplay and transformation; the idea of becoming a character and going to a convention as a ritual has always appealed to me.' She adds: 'Holly and I have been making costumes since we were kids . . . crafting with friends, becoming a character and having fun is what keeps us coming back.'

Wai in a Mad Hatter dress from the game *Alice: Madness Returns.*

Mei Wai

COSPLAYER

'Early on, cosplay wasn't easily accepted by everyone in China,' says Mei Wai, who's been cosplaying since 1999. 'People thought it was some kind of rebellion.'

In the last few years, though, cosplay has been commercialised for the masses there. There are now websites and magazines featuring cosplay photo shoots, with some *coser* (Chinese for cosplayers) even achieving online fame. 'You can say there is definitely a group of cosplayers who do it for the love,' says Wai, 'and one group that does it for the commercial aspects.'

Wai started cosplaying as a way to have fun and be creative. 'At that time, I had a lot of time on my hands, so I started focusing on cosplay,' she says. 'To me, the value of cosplay is in its creativity.'

Cosplayers do give some older, more traditional people in China pause for thought, especially when they parade around in public. While her family is supportive, not all are: some adults call this *hu nao* or 'trouble making', Wai says. 'To the elders, it looks like the cosplayers are partaking in an action that is inappropriate,' she explains, 'I mean, *cosers* look different, and so they open themselves up for elders to view them as different.'

Chiro as Dante from the *Devil May Cry* series.

Leon Chiro

COSPLAYER

Leon Chiro usually cosplays as characters with chiselled abs and big biceps. No wonder: Chiro, a former Calvin Klein underwear model, can effortlessly bring them to life. 'Remember,' he says, 'video games are not real. Cosplay is a way to make them real!'

But for Chiro, making these characters real requires sweat, hard work and expert posing. So when he isn't cosplaying, he's in the gym: 'I train a lot ... six days a week, with gymnastics, working out'. He also maintains a strict diet so he can stay in tip-top shape. But don't assume he's just some gym rat – Chiro says that he actually prefers sports or physical activities such as parkour: 'I don't even like the gym,' he admits.

Chiro discovered cosplay through modelling, after a friend, knowing that he loved video games, suggested that he give it a try. 'The similarities between cosplay and modelling are the use of interpretation, and the capacity to communicate feelings and emotions with your pose,' he explains. 'It's very important to know how to pose in cosplay.' Now, modelling is simply something Chiro does on the side; his hobby and his passion is cosplay.

Cosplay isn't the only thing motivating Chiro to stay in shape: the exercise and training he puts in also contribute to his future career plans, as the 23-year-old is currently studying physiotherapy and sports science in Rome. But when he's not studying, he spends weeks – sometimes months – putting together costumes of iconic male video game characters like *Devil May Cry*'s Dante or Tidius from *Final Fantasy X*. 'Exercise is part of my ordinary lifestyle, so I don't think I'll ever be out of shape,' says Chiro, adding that he always wants to look and feel his best. But if he ever let himself go, would he still cosplay? 'Even if I were in "bad shape" I would continue to cosplay ... but maybe not the really athletic stuff!'

Darrell Ardita

PHOTOGRAPHER

'I've always been a nerd at heart,' says photographer Darrell Ardita. 'I feel like photography has been that escape for me; it's my way of expressing myself as a gamer and comic fan.'

Ardita runs a studio called BGZ, which he founded over a decade ago, and spends much of the year on shoots for record labels, magazines and ad agencies. 'I actually started shooting cosplay before I shot anything else,' he says. 'The amount of work cosplayers put into their costumes continues to amaze me today. Their attention to detail and their skill at bringing some of my favourite characters to life inspires me to create along with them.'

Meredith Placko as Lara Croft
from the *Tomb Raider* series.

Tham as Queen Amidala from the film *Star Wars Episode I: The Phantom Menace*.

Meagan Marie as Gabriel Belmont from the video game *Castlevania: Lords of Shadow*.

Cosplay World

Mel Hoppe as Aela the Huntress from the video game *The Elder Scrolls V: Skyrim*.

Ryo Okita

COSPLAYER AND MAKER

Armour. Shields. Giant swords shaped like crab claws. Welcome to the world of Ryo Okita, who quit his desk job to make cosplay props and outfits full-time.

While in his early twenties, Okita befriended a cosplayer through the Internet and attended his first event. 'I looked at all the cosplayers, and it seemed like such fun,' he says. 'That's when I decided I wanted to make a costume myself.' The experience changed his life. He began to make more and more outfits, and his knack for producing props and complex costumes increased. He was spending his days sitting at a computer as a systems engineer, but what he really wanted to do was make cosplay kit all day long. Eventually, 'In 2010, I left my job and started crafting made-to-order props full-time.'

Okita doesn't just make things for himself and customers: he also offers tips and walkthroughs on his website for his complex props, which he hopes are 'useful to people around the world'. And not only is the website a way for Okita to share his costume crafting expertise, but it also gives him a chance to practice his English, as he handles his own translation work. 'I went to the US thirteen years ago, but since then, I haven't been outside Japan. Now I understand English better, and I'm happy to be able to communicate with English speakers. One day I'd like to go to a cosplay event abroad.'

Okita in armour from the *Monster Hunter* video games.

Natalia Voroninsky

COSPLAYER

Modern cosplay uses all kinds of materials and fabrics, but what happens when you live somewhere with no access to tools like foam sheeting or thermoplastic modelling material? As Natalia Voroninsky well knows, you have to get creative.

A journalist by trade, Voroninsky covers economics and business for a living in her native Russia. Her free time is spent creating intricate and impressive outfits – doubly impressive when you find out what she has to work with. 'Most of the materials available to European, American and Asian cosplayers are impossible to get hold of in Russia,' she says. 'So we have to make it up, literally, and use unusual materials.' 'Unusual' means stuff like construction foam, insulation materials and linoleum. 'It's impossible to get craft foam or Worbla here, so all that is left is to be envious.'

It's not only her materials that are a bit out-there: the characters Voroninsky picks are, too. She prefers it that way, making it a strong-point rather than a weakness. 'I don't always go with the mainstream. In my choice of costumes I don't always go by how complex it is, but how unique it is as well.'

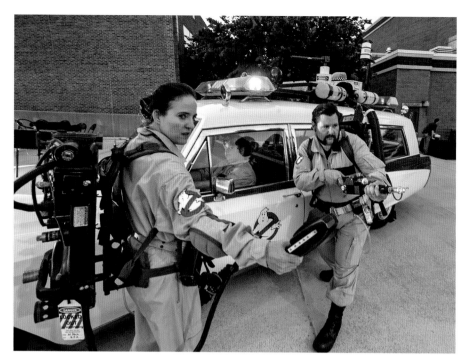

The Carolina Ghostbusters, with Geressy on the right.

The Carolina Ghostbusters' working Ecto-1 replica, built by Geressy.

M. Doc Geressy

COSPLAYER AND GHOSTBUSTER

Most *Ghostbusters* cosplay groups start small. Usually, creating their own Ecto-1, the iconic series' vehicle, is a distant dream. Not for M. Doc Geressy, though, a radio host and professor at the Carolina School of Broadcasting in Charlotte. 'I built the Ecto-1 first and then when people started wanting the car at events, I said, "Well, I guess I need to round up some Ghostbusters to go with this car!"'

A huge movie buff, Geressy first saw *Ghostbusters* as a kid, and has since seen it over a thousand times. But it wasn't until he found himself laid off with a severance package and divorced – in the same week – that he decided to build his own Ecto-1. In the films, the car is built from a 1959 Cadillac Miller-Meteor Ambulance. Instead, Geressy used a 1968 model that was unearthed in a Pennsylvania barn. 'A lot of people ask why I didn't use a '59 like in the movie, but only 88 of the limo-window ambulance-style Miller-Meteors were produced for the 1959 model year,' he says. After two and a half years of work, the car was ready to bust ghosts. Geressy reckons over $30,000 (£18,000) worth of work and parts has gone into his Ecto-1 tribute to date.

With a completed car, Geressy then needed some Ghostbusters, so he roped in friends from school, improv comedy groups and various conventions. Proton packs weighing 18 kg (40 lb) were assembled from scratch, and the Carolina Ghostbusters were born. 'People dress like their favourite characters for a variety of different reasons, but I think they all point back to a single reason: people want to be better,' he says.

For Geressy, the costume is more than fabric and props, 'it's a portal that allows a person to be as good-looking and as strong as the heroes they look up to and as confident and clever as the villains they admire. The costume allows a person to be someone else's hero, to make a connection with another human on a very core level, and to be the bridge that spans the gap between another person's imagination and their reality.'

The non-profit group of Carolina Ghostbusters spend around 70 or 80 days a year appearing at events, whether it's sci-fi cons, parades or charity fundraisers. They even have two ordained ministers as members, should people want to get married by a Ghostbuster and be whisked away in Ecto-1, which of course is 'way cooler than any limo'. Any money made from these appearances either goes back into maintaining the car and the Ghostbusting equipment – keeping a customised car like this in pristine running shape ain't cheap – or is donated to charity.

All of this is extraordinary enough but, believe it or not, the Carolina Ghostbusters are more than just cosplayers. Like their namesakes, they carry out paranormal investigations in the real world, using the same *Ghostbusters* equipment they've built for cosplay. The Ecto-1 doubles as their mobile command post. Does Geressy believe in ghosts? 'I'm probably one of the biggest sceptics you will meet. But I have witnessed a lot of events I can't explain. I don't know if they are ghosts per se, but there is definitely something else out there that exists that we don't entirely understand yet.'

Shina

COSPLAYER

You'd be forgiven for thinking Shina was a cosplay newcomer at just sixteen years old, but she's actually a seasoned veteran. 'I was about eleven when a friend said, "Hey can you come with me to the Japan Expo?" And I was like, "Why not!"'

At her first Japan Expo (a huge manga, anime and Japanese pop culture event held every year in Paris), Shina was overwhelmed by the cool cosplay on display. 'Months later I began my first cosplay, Yuffie Kisaragi from *Final Fantasy VII: Advent Children*,' she says. The experience gave her a huge rush. 'It wasn't very nice, but I put a lot of effort into it.'

After just one stint at Japan Expo, Shina's mind was made up. She decided to make more costumes, attend other cons and make more friends in the cosplay scene. 'It changed everything,' she says. 'Each time I talk about cosplay with non-cosplayers, they wonder how it's even possible – and in a good way! I got five of my friends into cosplay.' Not bad for a kid still in high school.

Shina as Akemi Homura from the anime
Puella Magi Madoka Magica.

Kokis as Optimus Prime.

Kokis as a T-800 from the film *Terminator*.

Cosplay World

Peter Kokis

COSPLAYER

Peter Kokis is a former attack helicopter pilot who now performs under the name Brooklyn RobotWorks, building elaborate suits based on famous robots which he wears to events, promotions and conventions. He calls his creations 'living sculptures'. To date, he's made over eight of them, all sporting New York licence plates that read 'BROOKLYN'.

'My journey from serious and stiff professional to artist started with a joke a few years ago, which became a hobby, and then became a rediscovery of an artistic side in me that had been suppressed when I joined the military.' Kokis describes how with 'little mechanical ability' and drawing on his experience as a pilot, he learned to make his metal outfits last, while still 'giving them room for improvement' – which he does, and does often. His very first costume, an Optimus Prime suit, initially weighed 20 kg (45 lb). Now, after eleven revisions, it weighs a massive 60 kg (130 lb).

These revisions are the result of months of hard work, not just in putting the outfits together but in finding the parts. Unlike many other cosplayers, Kokis doesn't so much build his suits from scratch as cobble them together out of hundreds – sometimes thousands – of everyday items. 'My art is to replicate these characters using ordinary and readily available items,' he says. Whether it's the hardware store, a sporting goods retailer or even a pet shop, he finds inspiration everywhere. 'At first, I used existing items from nearby stores just out of convenience, but then it became "my thing". I seek out shapes and complexity in simple things.'

All of Kokis's cosplay pieces share something in common, with names like 'Brooklyn Terminator', 'Brooklyn Bumblebee' and 'Brooklyn Alien'. 'My "brand" came from a simple thing: the use of a small $3 tourist gift shop licence plate stamped "BROOKLYN" at the Coney Island Mermaid Parade,' he explains. 'During the parade I kept hearing people making comments about the plate, and I had a "eureka!" moment. So, I became Brooklyn RobotWorks.' There's nothing quite like doing your hometown proud . . . with enormous robots.

Darshelle Stevens

PHOTOGRAPHER

'For quite a while I'd been struggling to fill a void I felt was present in my photographs,' says photographer Darshelle Stevens. 'Cosplay photography made me realise that it was the subjects in the photos that I needed, to really help push the envelope.'

For Stevens, cosplayers and the characters they portray give her images a narrative that she feels other photos are missing. Though she only got into taking pictures a few years ago, she now works full-time as a photographer and photo editor. A big gamer, she's found the cosplay scene to be not just something she wants to be a part of, but something that inspires her work. 'Everyone involved in the cosplay community is super-passionate about what they do, and being surrounded by that creative love really helps drive me.'

Cosplay has given Stevens's photos more than just a story to tell. 'Not too many people know this, but my "day job" is editing wedding photos,' she says. 'Seems boring to some, but I love the balance of getting to edit the more "human" photos, and then indulging in my personal work. I get to stimulate all corners of my creative mind.'

Lyz Brickley as Lightning from the video game series *Final Fantasy*.

Art is a personal journey that we merely share with others. If you don't love your work, that most likely means you're not doing it for yourself. When you stay true to you, and the things you love most, then everything else kind of falls into place.

Lyz Brickley as Garrett from the video game series *Thief*.

Ralf Zimmerman and Laura Jansen as barbarians from the video game series *Diablo*.

Marie as Warrior Wonder Woman.

Cutting a template for the helm.

Assembling the pattern layers.

The completed, blood-stained outfit.

Meagan Marie

Making a quality cosplay outfit that looks great in a photo or at a convention isn't easy. The amount of work that goes into a good costume is remarkable: designing, drawing, sewing, prop creation – all of which must be considered long before the cosplayer dons the outfit, and which need to be perfected to bring the character to life. Here, cosplay superstar Meagan Marie takes us through the complete process of designing and constructing an outfit, as she transforms into Wonder Woman.

Becoming Warrior Wonder Woman

This was a dream project in every sense of the word. As is true for many, Wonder Woman was the first female superhero I was introduced to in the world of comics. She holds a really special place in my fandom, and while I love the stars, stripes and satin tights of classic Wonder Woman, I've always been drawn to her origins as one of the Amazons. I pictured Wonder Woman as a warrior first and foremost, and wanted to bring my specific vision of her to life.

I recruited the extremely talented artist Tess Fowler to help me put an original spin on a classic character. Our collaboration kicked off with lots of research. I sifted through dozens of incarnations of Wonder Woman, both official and fan creations. I knew I wanted a gladiator-style skirt and corset,

a sword, shield and bracers. I also wanted a half-helm and cape, the latter having the added benefit of modesty. I envisioned practical footwear: flat sandals. Armed with my notes and a slew of reference materials, Tess turned around an initial design that was drawn directly from my imagination. After a few minor adjustments and a quick colour pass, Warrior Wonder Woman was born.

A shopping trip to a leather supply shop was in order to kick off the costume. My friend and leatherworking expert Tom Ignatius came along to ensure I picked out the right hides for the project, as I needed different finishes for the skirt and the corset. I grabbed a load of blue leather dye as well as a few dozen decorative conchos, both for the tips of the skirt and as finishing touches for each armour piece.

Armed with my supplies, I began the project with a massive amount of patterning on paper. I calculated out the amount of coverage I wanted from the skirt on both my front and back to determine the width and length each piece should be. After confirming the fit on paper, I traced each piece on to the leather, cutting it with a straight-edge rotary blade. Once all the pieces were cut out, I began dyeing the leather. Each piece needed two to three coats on both the front and back to get the even, deep blue I wanted.

While waiting for each coat to dry, I set about patterning and cutting Wonderflex (an easy-to-use thermoplastic) pieces for the ornamentation at the bottom of each skirt piece. This was tedious, but not particularly hard. After giving them a quick coat of paint, each armoured tip was attached to the leather skirt pieces with brass fasteners. I also added a concho to the tip of each skirt piece.

The armour came next, and once again I made everything as paper patterns first, to ensure the pieces were properly sized to my measurements before switching to the plastic. The armour consists of multiple layers of Wonderflex aligned on top of each other, with a thin layer used as trim around the sides. I bonded all the pieces together while flat to achieve maximum adhesion, then shaped them to fit my arms and legs. I used a soldering iron to smooth out the edges and give it a more polished look. The helm, eagle, belt and hand guards were made much the same way: pattern on paper, transfer to Wonderflex, heat and bond, shape, and then repeat for another layer. Once all the pieces were done, I used a grommet tool to make holes for leather laces. I also lined each piece of armour with self-adhesive craft foam to act as a buffer between the Wonderflex and my skin.

I bought a wooden sword to ensure it was safe for conventions. I roughed it up quite a bit and added leather to the grip. I then set to work on the shield, which comprises a wooden bar-stool top, an ornamental eagle from a necklace, a plate from a candle holder, bisected Christmas ornaments, and leftover leather. Per my personal cosplay philosophy, I always look for form instead of function, and was super-happy to find all of the above while wandering aimlessly up and down the aisles of hardware and craft stores. Prior to painting the armour and props, I proceeded to distress everything. I used my soldering iron as well as various heavy-duty files and sandpaper to add realistic-looking weapon grazes.

Knowing that I'd be using hammered metal paint, I skipped priming all my armour with gesso, something I recommend otherwise. The base of each piece of armour is silver. I then used a muted hammered gold as accent on the trim. I used a much brighter silver in the damaged recesses of the armour, making it look like a raw layer of metal. The final touch was a bit of dirt and stage blood, sprayed out of a bottle and allowed to drip down each piece and dry.

With the armour done, the next step was to tackle the corset. Having never made one, I was a bit apprehensive about attempting it on my own. Luckily, Tom is also a master corset maker and offered to help with the process and let me use his industrial sewing machine. We looked through his huge collection of corset patterns to decide on the general style and shape, modifying it slightly to have a sweetheart neckline. I played assistant in the corset's construction, tracing and cutting out all the pieces while Tom sewed them together. I did sew a handful of the pieces towards the end, though, under his watchful eye, to ensure I learned the proper technique for the future. Once it was finished, I attached the skirt pieces to the corset with rivets – a long and painful process when you're exhausted and have horrendous depth perception.

Next came the cape. I'd ordered some fantastic trim in contrasting colours from overseas, and attached it to a simple solution for a quick cape: an oversized circular tablecloth with the middle cut out. Once the trim was attached I put the entire thing in a bath of coffee and tea to age it. It was then attached to my costume with grommets and the matching conchos. With everything finished I took to the leather and cape with a cheese grater for additional wear and tear, and used black and brown hairspray to dirty it up a bit.

The final touch was the wig. I went for a slightly wavy, shoulder-length look, adding a braid to each side of my face for an ornamental and utilitarian style – the braids keeping stray hairs from obstructing my vision. I made sure to dirty myself up, too, to match my attire, using the hairspray on my skin as well. The process involves diluting the hairspray for an initial pass, wiping it on with my hands; a second layer is then stippled on with a sponge for more distinct patterns of dirt.

At the risk of looking silly, I pushed myself quite hard to look aggressive and intimidating during the various photo shoots I organised for Warrior Wonder Woman. While there may be a few giggle-worthy images floating around of me failing spectacularly at looking tough, I think the risk paid off, as many of the images capture the warrior spirit I was so eagerly aiming for.

Costume concept sketch
by Tess Fowler.

Marie in the completed Warrior Wonder Woman costume.

Mo Meinhart as spider queen Arachnia.

Judith Stephens

PHOTOGRAPHER

By day, Judith Stephens is an associate producer at Marvel where, among many other responsibilities, she is their website's cosplay blogger. 'It's through my work at Marvel that I have been able to grow so much as a cosplay photographer,' says Stephens. 'My co-workers are incredibly interested in what I do on the weekends and supportive of my "hobby", which allows me to travel frequently to conventions and events, including one year when I was able to attend fifteen cons!'

Stephens's high school days were spent dressing up with friends in goth or punk gear for photo shoots in and around Detroit, and evenings were spent in darkrooms, developing the photos. This was before the digital era, so they didn't know if they'd got the shots they wanted until the film was actually developed.

While studying photography at Parsons The New School for Design in New York City, Stephens got into anime, manga and, in turn, cosplay. 'Besides the exciting aspect of taking photos of favourite characters, it was the cosplay community that really drew me in,' she says. 'As a photographer, the ability to photograph fantastical characters and creators and meld them into the vision I see in my head is pretty much a dream come true.'

Her first subjects were new cosplay pals she had met around the city, who were only too happy to hit up cons with her and pose for pics. 'Those first photos were also my first real foray into digital,' she says. 'As I learned how to photograph cosplayers I was also learning how to manage a digital camera.' Cosplay became the perfect way for Stephens to explore her love of bright, vivid colours. 'When I first began documenting the cosplay community, I really tried using my photographs to summarise the immense world we've created for ourselves. Along the way I realised that that in itself was a job – one I wouldn't be able to tackle in its entirety – but I hope that my photographs are a glimpse into this cosplay family I've become a part of.'

Mostflogged as Noriko, Namiko101 as Amano, and Sky-too-high as Jung, all from the anime series *Gunbuster*.

Cosplay photography is, for me, a bunch of friends coming together to do something fun. The 'real world' requires a bit more strategy than that.

Namiko101 as Panty from the manga and animated series *Panty & Stocking with Garterbelt*.

Stan Lee and friends at Dragon Con 2012 in Atlanta, Georgia.

Cosplay World

Danquish as Sam Gideon from *Vanquish*.

Danquish

COSPLAYER

When browsing the Internet and attending conventions, it can seem like nearly every cosplayer is female. Guys are fans too, though, so what's the deal? 'I think perhaps the reason you might not see that many men in the scene is that they may think they don't have what it takes,' says Canadian cosplayer Danquish. 'Or maybe they're intimidated because there are so many women in cosplay, thus making them feel vastly outnumbered.'

Danquish enjoys cosplay because he loves bringing his favourite characters to life. 'I have attended numerous cons and have seen plenty of men executing some astonishing recreations of characters, and it's just awesome. Male cosplayers are definitely out there, and they're a very talented lot.'

Cosplaying primarily as video game characters, in particular *Vanquish*'s Sam Gideon (it's where he got his stage name), Danquish doesn't just dress for himself: he does it as a homage to the developers who made those games possible. 'Each character I choose to cosplay has significant meaning to me. When I finally complete a cosplay, it's not only because I enjoy the character or game it represents; it's my small way of saying thanks to the character's creators for making something I love so much – enough that I wanted to recreate it in real life.'

Rana McAnear

COSPLAYER

Rana McAnear is different. Where every other cosplayer has to spend weeks (if not months) toiling to resemble a character they love, McAnear looks like one every day, as soon as she gets out of bed. Well, save for the blue skin and the extraterrestrial hair, that is.

'I'm a little spoiled, cosplaying as myself,' says McAnear, one of the stars of the *Mass Effect* video games. Her face served as the in-game model for Samara and Morinth, two of the series' Asari aliens.

Having 'played' the roles professionally for a number of years, you might think she'd be sick of donning the Asaris' trademark blue skin and armour, but her love of the characters has instead fuelled an interest in cosplay. McAnear, who by day works in the film industry, now attends conventions all over the US, bringing Samara and Morinth to life in a way few can match. 'I love the people I have met through this adventure,' she says of her cosplay travels, 'everyone is so kind and welcoming.'

Jibrii Ransom

COSPLAYER

Who is that masked man? Jibrii Ransom, that's who. Whether he's cosplaying as Spawn or Skeletor, Ransom enjoys the element of mystery his cosplay disguise provides. 'By day I am a typical geek, but during conventions I am this masked cosplayer,' he reveals. 'And it is an amazing feeling to be a mystery to other people. Also . . . I really like wearing capes.'

Family members helped foster Ransom's love for comics from an early age: even as a small child his cousins or grandfather would read them to him or share their favourite stories. By the time he was in high school, Ransom and his friends were bonding over Marvel and DC adventures and hanging out in comic book shops. His first cosplaying effort was a store-bought Halloween costume and was, in his words, 'so bad'. However, he enjoyed the experience enough that he later taught himself how to sew, practising over and over until he became skilled enough to start making his own outfits.

'I feel that cosplay is a lot like acting,' says Ransom, who studied acting and film-making in college. 'When you cosplay, you become that character. You have to live as that character, and consider how would they talk, pose, move and act. I feel that is just as important as accuracy to detail of a character.'

As any good actor will tell you, it's necessary to really understand the character you are playing. Thus, whether they're from comics or video games, Ransom won't cosplay characters he isn't incredibly familiar with. Until recently, most of his cosplay has been as masked characters from comics: 'Most of them have no superpowers, but trained to make themselves better and stronger so they could be superheroes or vigilantes.'

Ransom as the Marvel Comics character Moon Knight.

Crystal Graziano

COSPLAYER

'I started going to the San Diego Comic-Con in 2003,' says Crystal Graziano, admitting that 'cosplayers initially weirded me out'. It took a couple of years' exposure to warm her up, but by 2005 Graziano was stepping into her first outfit. 'My first costume was of Aeris from *Final Fantasy VII*, with no wig, and while my costume was terrible, the people I met through cosplay were so cool that I was hooked. It was a really great way to make friends with people who shared the same interests as me.'

One of those people was Todd, her husband, who she sometimes cosplays alongside. Given that some of her outfits can be on the revealing side, jealousy might be expected to rear its ugly head, but Graziano says that the pair actually work together really well. 'When it comes to cosplay, we generally just try to focus on portraying the characters. If I'm cosplaying a character with a sexy element, I'll just portray that too! Todd and I are very secure in our relationship, and I do my best to keep even the sexy pictures classy.'

From a reluctant beginning, Graziano has been lucky enough to reach the pinnacle of cosplay, becoming one of the few given the chance to turn their passion into a profession. Employed by video game studio Red 5 in 2012, she was able to spend an entire year cosplaying professionally, modelling for the company's game *Firefall* but also, importantly, having her personal work paid for. 'The money was of course wonderful and helped get nicer materials for the costumes, but I especially enjoyed the critiques from my hero Steve Wang.'

As part of the deal, Wang, a Hollywood special effects legend who has designed and built creatures for movies like *Predator* and *Hellboy*, was on hand to lend Graziano costuming advice. This is the kind of help most cosplayers can only dream of. 'There are a few people who are against getting money for cosplay at all, but in general people were very supportive,' she says of the experience. 'It's really great to see video game companies acknowledge and support the cosplay community in such a way.'

Graziano as Ivy from the *Soulcalibur* video game series.

Crystal Graziano

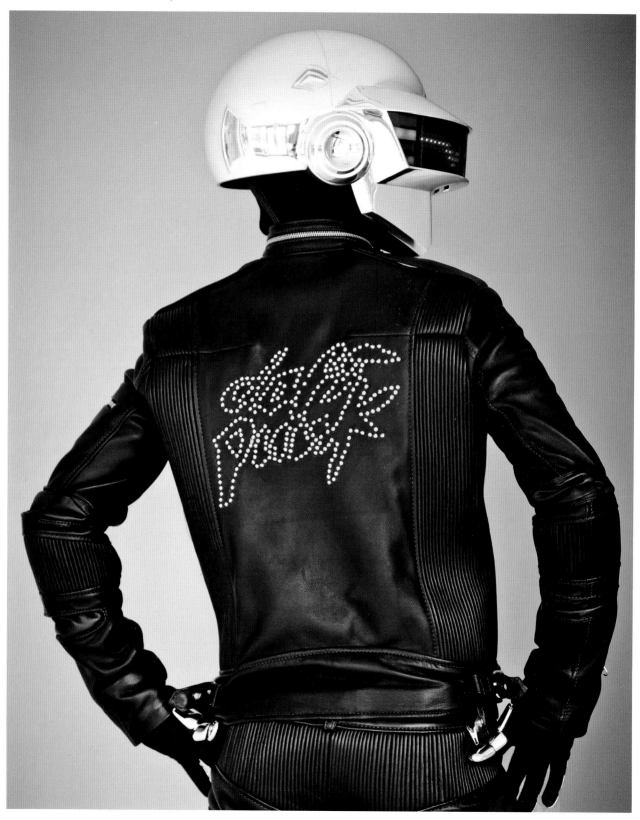

Bill Doran

COSPLAYER AND MAKER

In 2012 Bill Doran kissed his desk job goodbye and went full-time with his business, Punished Props. 'Before this I published video on the Internet,' he explains. 'It was a good job, very secure, yet terribly boring! The decision wasn't even that hard. I had way more commissions piled up than I had time to finish, so I took the plunge.'

Doran's work is driven by his love of video games, since that's what first got him into building replica weapons and armour. 'The idea of ripping a weapon from the virtual world into the real world was what inspired me to take this path. Once people started seeing me do those kinds of projects, that's all they asked for.'

As a cosplayer himself, Doran knows that it's often the accessories that really 'make' an outfit, providing its finishing touches: 'Consider *Final Fantasy*'s Cloud without his gigantic Buster Sword. The costume doesn't carry as much majesty without the prop.'

In addition to building gear for cosplayers, he also takes commissions from collectors, who pay him to recreate their favourite weapons, helmets and shields so they can display them in their homes and offices. Though it wasn't his original career choice, Doran says Punished Props is the only job he's got the passion to do every day and the drive to make succeed as a business. 'I get up and build space guns every single day and I think that's just about the coolest thing ever!'

Tasha

COSPLAYER

The Spiral Cats started out making video games. Now, they're South Korea's most famous professional cosplay team. Tasha, one of the group's key members, began cosplaying in university. 'We were college students all majoring in art, so it was mostly out of enjoyment in the beginning,' she says.

Giving up making games to take up cosplay full-time wasn't an easy decision. 'Even as late as 2011, which wasn't that long ago, cosplay in Korea was considered something that junior high and high school kids did for fun,' says Tasha. Now, things are different. Working with gaming giants like Blizzard, Nexon and Microsoft to bring iconic characters to life has helped Spiral Cats change the image of cosplay at home. 'All of our costumes and props are made in-house,' Tasha explains. 'Our office has a photo studio, make-up chairs, costumes and a prop production area, which allows all of us to work under one roof. Think of it as a space dedicated to cosplay.' The group's headquarters is now in Seoul's ritzy Gangnam Apgujeong neighbourhood.

Despite breaking out into the cosplay world, Spiral Cats are plotting their next move, and are keen to return to their roots by developing a Spiral Cats game, as well as rolling out teams in other countries. 'Having teams around the world with the same name, and being in friendly cosplay competition, is something we'd like to achieve one day,' Tasha says. 'It's all dreams right now, but we are going to use this as our motivation and work hard.'

Tasha as Maga from the online role-playing game *Monarch*.

Tasha as Hotaru from the online role-playing game *Cyphers*.

Tasha

Ariana Barouk as Silk Spectre from the graphic novel *Watchmen*.

Jay Tablante

PHOTOGRAPHER

'When I started shooting these photos, I was just concerned with bringing out the childhood fantasies in my head,' says Jay Tablante. He got interested in photography while in high school, but it wasn't until college that Tablante studied it formally. He also undertook an apprenticeship with a professional photographer, learning the tricks of the trade, and began shooting some friends who aspired to become models. By the time he was a college senior he'd got more serious about the art, and was hired to shoot a fashion billboard.

'Over the years, I found myself hanging out at more comic book conventions than photography-related events,' says Tablante. 'Artists, particularly comic book artists, have a hyper-realistic perspective on creating images. It made me think that if I could find a means to translate their imagination into the realm of photography, perhaps I might have a chance in making my images unique.'

Cosplay was the next step. For Tablante, cosplay photography helped him fulfil his childhood dream of seeing heroes and villains come to life. 'I love both photography and pop culture,' he says. 'Cosplay photography became the perfect means of combining both in a single endeavour.' Tablante studied video game design, and never actually planned on being a professional photographer – but photography has become more than just a way for

him to explore the pop culture he's absorbed his whole life. 'Since I can't draw, cosplay is my means of expressing my imagination without having to hold a pencil.'

Rhian Ramos Howell as Rogue from *X-Men*.

Faus Ongtengco, Natalia Santiago, Ashley Gosiengfiao, Alodia Gosiengfiao and Maria Dolonius as characters from *Alice in Wonderland*; inspired by the Tim Burton film, Tablante named this scene 'The Tea After Party'.

Cosplay World

A picture may be bound by four physical frames and a temporal moment, but that doesn't mean a viewer's imagination is also limited the same way. You have to cater to their innate need to understand things in anything they encounter. Our minds work by connecting information based on experiences.

Simon Melmeth

COSPLAYER

When Simon Melmeth is Simon Melmeth, he's a career firefighter and a married father-of-two with a degree in nuclear medicine. When he's TK-7543, however, he's a walking *Star Wars* contradiction: an Imperial Stormtrooper who's one of the good guys.

Melmeth is a member of the 501st Legion, an all-volunteer formal organisation for *Star Wars* costuming, with thousands of members across the globe. But they don't just dress up for fun – they also do it to help people in need. 'The Legion seeks to promote interest in *Star Wars* through the building and wearing of quality costumes, and to facilitate the use of these costumes for *Star Wars*-related events as well as contributions to the local community through costumed charity and volunteer work,' the group's charter states. Melmeth's favourite events are always the hospital visits: 'Being able to put a smile on the faces of some children who are sick or injured and in need of long-term care is the most rewarding thing,' he says.

While the 501st's members are considered by many to be cosplayers, that's not a universal label. You won't see the word 'cosplay' anywhere on their website, for example. 'I think the 501st means different things to different people,' Melmeth says. 'I know many people that would think of us as cosplayers but, personally, I enjoy the charity side of it more than the actual making of the costumes.'

Melmeth almost always dresses up not as one of the many *Star Wars* heroes, but its villains. 'Most of the good guys such as Luke are "face" characters and, unless you really resemble the actors, the costume just doesn't look right,' he says. 'With the bad guys such as the Stormtroopers, you can look like you literally stepped out of the screen. Plus, since your face is hidden behind a helmet, people can be less self-conscious knowing that no one can see them. There's also the undeniable cool factor of the scary, faceless minion. And, chicks dig the bad boys.'

The 501st Legion as characters from *Star Wars*.

Hagopian with her colleague Paul Tofani during a re-enactment.

Julie Hagopian

HISTORICAL RE-ENACTOR AND COSPLAYER

'Re-enacting is a way to make history tangible for modern folk,' says Julie Hagopian, a member of the 5th New York Regiment, a group who describe themselves as 'living historians'. 'It's easy to read about George Washington crossing the Delaware River at midnight on Christmas Day, but it's only when you actually suit up in appropriate clothing, feel the cold chill of the wind as you board the boat, carrying your musket and gear, and tread in Washington's footsteps, that you can truly appreciate history.'

A history graduate who swordfights, attends Renaissance fairs and who undertook an apprenticeship as a seamstress in order to build her historically accurate clothing, Hagopian and her comrades in the 5th dress up as historical figures, stage mock battles and educate the public about life in years gone by.

Re-enactment isn't cosplay, despite the similarities. Julie does cosplay though, having been introduced to anime like *Cowboy Bebop* and *Hetalia*, so she's in the perfect position to speak about what the two fields have – and don't have – in common. 'Although from the outside cosplay and re-enacting seem very close, I would have to say they're still different.' She explains: 'Cosplay is recreating something from fictional entertainment out of admiration. Re-enacting involves historical research, oftentimes from multiple sources, to realistically represent what the past was like and embody it.'

Another key difference is that, while cosplayers can use whatever materials they like to make their costumes, re-enactors must put together their 'period-appropriate dress' with materials that were in use in the period being represented – which may be hundreds of years ago. But that doesn't mean the two subcultures lack similarities: 'From a theatrical viewpoint, re-enactors try to jump into character to portray a role or persona, often to benefit the public by teaching them,' says Hagopian. 'Cosplayers also have specific characters they embody. This dedication to accuracy is a common thread.'

Allen Amis

COSPLAYER

Boba Fett, one of the most iconic *Star Wars* characters, has come full circle. In 2011, cosplayer Allen Amis met artist Clinton Felker at the Devastation gaming con, held in Phoenix, Arizona. 'Clinton had done an art piece of his concept Samurai Boba Fett that I just fell in love with,' says Amis. 'I fell in love with it so much I just had to build it.'

Amis has been into costuming since the 1990s, when he began fighting in the Society for Creative Anachronism (a group that studies and recreates pre-17th-century European cultures). 'It was there that I learned how to make armour that could stand intense fighting on the field,' he says. He then joined the *Star Wars* costuming group the Mandalorian Mercs, which is a sister group to the *Star Wars* cosplay outfit the 501st Legion. There he met his

costuming partner Anabel Martinez, with whom he's delved deeper into the *Star Wars* universe.

As Amis points out, for *Star Wars*, George Lucas was heavily influenced by the samurai films of Akira Kurosawa. Boba Fett, meanwhile, was loosely based on Clint Eastwood's lone gunslinger in Sergio Leone's classic westerns, the first of which, *Fistful of Dollars* (1964), was based on Kurosawa's *ronin* film *Yojimbo*, made a few years earlier. Jeremy Bulloch, the actor who played Boba Fett, took his cue from Eastwood's character in those spaghetti westerns. 'So Samurai Boba Fett just brought everything 360,' says Amis. 'I think Boba's early appeal was hugely based on these questions: who is he, where did he come from, how did he get that dent on his helmet, what's his story?'

Benjamin 'Beethy' Koelewijn

PHOTOGRAPHER

Benjamin 'Beethy' Koelewijn says not many people see his photos and think, 'Boy, what an amazing shot.' 'They're more inclined to admire the cosplayer, since that's the person in the photo,' he says, knowing that while he's been equally responsible for the final result, the part he played is probably less obvious. 'At the end of the day I don't mind; I'm happy, since people see my photos regardless.'

For Beethy, there's a load of different factors that make cosplay photography appealing, from experimentation to get the background right, to getting the correct feel for the character, to simply working with talented and generous cosplayers.

As one of the world's most prolific and prominent cosplay photographers, you'd probably think he takes his stunning photos using expensive equipment, but that's actually not the case. 'Years ago, due to some severe financial difficulties, I had to sell off all my pro gear,' says Beethy. 'It was all very high-end stuff: lighting gear, $3,000 lenses, the works.' For over two years now, he's been working with one of the cheapest digital SLR cameras around, and one of the cheapest lenses you can find, too, proving it's not how much the equipment costs but who is using it that matters. 'Equipment is irrelevant for the most part,' he says. 'You can still achieve great results using minimal gear. The only special technique would be my focus to build a real connection with my subject.'

Yasemin Arslan as Lilith from the video game series *Borderlands*.

Princess Bee as Harley Quinn from *Batman*.

Yasemin Arslan as Lilith from the video game series *Borderlands*.

I think postwork is almost a must with cosplay photography. Some of the best cosplay photographers in the world employ heavy use of Photoshop. It's what really finishes off the image. Most photos in art galleries and on the covers of magazines are also heavily edited; it's an integral part of photography now. But I'm not against not using any postwork at all. As long as the end result is solid, it doesn't matter how they did it.

Nadleeh as Sheryl Nome from the anime series *Macross Frontier*.

Thunderbolt as a trainer from the *Pokémon* video game series.

Aicosu

COSPLAYERS

Sheila and Sylar are a cosplaying couple who perform under the name Aicosu. Sheila discovered cosplay in 2007 and decided to give it a try so she could bring her favourite characters to life. 'I discovered cosplay around the same time, but I didn't try it until I met Sheila two years later, at a convention,' remembers Sylar. 'Sheila was cosplaying and I wasn't. I had always wanted to try it, but she's the one who really encouraged me and got me excited . . . But really, we were both more interested in dating each other at the time.'

It wasn't until after they became a couple that they decided to cosplay together, as two characters from their favourite anime at the time, *Code Geass*. The pair have been cosplaying for over four years now, and to date they have over 90 costumes under their belts.

Sheila studied illustration and costume design at the prestigious Rhode Island School of Design, learning skills that now come in very handy for making cosplay outfits. 'As an artist and specifically a designer, I have experience in breaking down forms and in composition,' says Sheila. 'So figuring out the pieces of a costume just by eyeballing it is natural to me. I also have a better eye for proportion than most, which can be very important when determining sizes of armour or props in relation to a person.'

Sylar is studying at the Academy of Art University in San Francisco, and hopes to become a voice actor. Growing up, he loved imitating his favourite TV and video game characters. 'Cosplay also gave me the opportunity to challenge myself with new voices,' he says. 'Being able to voice your characters is a great way to set you apart from other cosplayers. It's something I've used to add more to the experience of cosplay.'

With one of them still a student, the couple is committed to a long-distance relationship. 'Cosplay and conventions are definitely a great excuse to get together and see each other,' says Sylar. 'It's nice to have someone to lean on, vent to, and share experiences with in this crazy hobby,' says Sheila. 'Especially when things get complicated. It makes the difficult times better and the amazing times absolutely unforgettable.'

Little Wren

COSPLAYER AND BURLESQUE DANCER

Burlesque entertainer and cosplayer Little Wren's art forms of choice involve creating and portraying a character. 'A lot of work goes into burlesque costume design and choreography, much like any cosplay masquerade competition,' she says. The key difference? Burlesque adds a sexy twist.

Little Wren was already an acclaimed burlesque performer when she discovered cosplay, and she had also long been fascinated with dressing up and donning costumes for Halloween and parties. At Dragon Con in 2008, she fell in love with all the wonderful costumes she saw. 'Seeing that I could dress up at many other times of the year and be around other people who enjoyed anime, games and sci-fi like I did was just an incredible discovery!'

She learned about costuming through performing on the Atlanta burlesque scene, picking up sewing tips from costumer Pinky Shear and getting performance advice from fellow burlesque performer The Chameleon Queen. 'To wow a crowd, everything is important – from the moment you walk on to the stage to the very last sequin on your pasty,' says Little Wren. Similarly, in cosplay, 'You want the end result to be an expression of how much you love the character. Researching, buying materials, sewing, crafting, and even just leaving the house are all huge investments in a cosplayer's life.'

'Burlesque is about the tease,' says Little Wren. 'Sure, it's still stripping, but it's not just a sparkly dress coming off.' For her, it might be Hermione casting a love spell, for example, or the Mad Hatter mixing herself into a glistening pot of tea. Character and costume are intertwined. 'Even before women of burlesque began to peel off their clothing, they were mostly categorised by their outlandish attire. The costumes are a huge part of creating your character and telling your story.'

Courtney Morelock

COSPLAYER

For Courtney Morelock, nothing beats the moment when she first sees herself in a finished costume. 'When you first look at yourself in the mirror, you are just like, "Wow",' she says. 'The moment you are no longer you and you are able to embody another character . . . it feels really cool. It's an out-of-body experience.' The same goes for walking around a convention, especially with a group of friends, says Morelock, whose cosplay name is Courtoon. 'You really get into a different mindset,' and the outfit enables the wearer to become the character: the costume makes the cosplayer.

But cosplay isn't always high-fives and smiles. Morelock reminds us of one of the pitfalls of the pastime: as much fun as it can be, people's expectations can be unrealistic, and sometimes things can get mean. 'All cosplayers are bound to face a few bad moments in the community,' she says. 'I've been attacked many times – called ugly, fat and a wide variety of other colourful words. It really hurts at first, and still does to this day, but as long as you are happy with yourself that's all that should matter.'

I think that Photoshop is a wonderful tool to enhance your photographs. It is just like in the old days, in the darkroom, where people would dodge and burn photographic material or use contrast filters to get the best and most dramatic effect in their shots.

Cynthia Veekens

PHOTOGRAPHER

'I have never been a "normal" photographer,' says Cynthia Veekens. 'I was always looking for things out of the ordinary, subjects that stood out from a crowd.'

While most people get into cosplay through fandom, the Dutch photographer's journey has been a more artistic one. She had long been interested in theatrical costumes and the entire process that goes into making them. Then, 'when I started to visit fantasy fairs in Holland I got interested in the outfits people made. So for me, cosplay photography is more like a form of appreciation and admiration for the artists themselves.'

While aware that much of the credit for a successful photo shoot should go to the cosplayer due to the time and effort that goes into making a costume, Veekens reminds us that the photographer does more than just click a button. 'If done well, a photographer will put their heart and soul into the photograph to try and make the character come to life,' she says. 'In a way, you have to think as the cosplayer would, try to think how the character would react to their surroundings, anticipate that, try to see the perfect light and then: click, you take the shot.'

Despite her skill in capturing other people's craft, cosplay isn't something she partakes in herself. 'I am not a cosplayer, nor do I own any costumes,' says Veekens. 'The only time I've come close is riding around on my horse, yelling, and imagining I was Xena the Warrior Princess! I think cosplay, when taken seriously, is a form of art, and I love anything related to art.'

Akira Konomi

COSPLAYER AND VOICE ACTOR

Akira Konomi trained to become an Olympic skier, but ended up a cosplay champ. Konomi's childhood was spent on the slopes of Hokkaido, Japan, as a slalom skier; whenever she wasn't practising, though, she was reading manga and watching anime.

At age seventeen, however, an injury cruelly robbed her of her sporting dreams. Enter cosplay. While in junior high school Konomi attended a comic book event, where she witnessed cosplay for the first time. 'It was like being at Disneyland and seeing Mickey Mouse,' she says. Having her picture taken with her favourite characters, like Vincent from *Final Fantasy VII*, she initially didn't realise that these were die hard fans, instead figuring they were hired help. 'I thought it was amazing you could show your love for a character using your entire body,' says Konomi. 'If you simply say you like a certain character, the reaction is, "Oh, that's nice." But if you cosplay as that character, people can actually see how much you love that character, by noticing all the small details in your costume and the way you pose.'

Once she found out people were dressing up in those outfits for fun, Konomi was hooked. 'If I could draw,' she says, 'I would probably draw my favourite characters. But I can't, so I cosplay.' For her, cosplay became a way to show not only her admiration and creativity but also her gratitude to the artists, writers and creators behind the stories and characters.

Konomi doesn't just think about the character but tries to imagine the world they live in – like method acting, only for cosplay. 'I try to remember certain feelings, like when I'm really angry,' she says. 'Then, I use that while I'm cosplaying to evoke a particular character.' For example, when she cosplayed as Naruto, the noodle-loving ninja, she ate ramen five times a week to try to understand the character. For other cosplay, she may work out to change her physical appearance.

Konomi has now been cosplaying for half her life. She has represented Japan at the World Cosplay Summit and has appeared at cosplay events throughout Asia. Her photos have been shown at art galleries, and she even spearheads a cosplay performance troupe that brings anime and manga to life via dinner theatre. Her performance of football anime *Inazuma Eleven* was so good that the show's producers hired her as a voice actor for the character Napa Ladam, making her the first cosplayer to make the leap to professional voice acting.

Konomi as Napa Ladam from the video game and anime *Inazuma Eleven*.

Konomi as the virtual idol Hatsune Miku
from *Vocaloid*.

Konomi as Sheryl Nome from the mecha anime
series *Macross Frontier*.

Cosplay World

Akira Konomi

Sewing is still considered to be a very feminine form of art all over the world. Your male friends might make fun of you if you say that you sew costumes of cartoon characters as a hobby. It's also very hard to even try and compete against boobs and butts on the Internet. Sadly, it's difficult for male cosplayers to get the same amount of attraction as females do.

Janne 'Elffi' Rusanen

COSPLAYER

Some cosplayers are lucky if they ever make it to a major convention like Dragon Con or Comic-Con. Others, like Janne Rusanen, aka Elffi, are bona fide international jetsetters. 'Nine months into 2013, I had visited eight countries for twelve conventions across three continents,' says Elffi, who is known for bringing heroic male characters to life.

That's impressive enough, but for Elffi, a student who works part-time both as a cab driver and an undertaker, the best part is that it doesn't cost him a cent. Shows around the world line up to pay him to attend and judge their competitions. 'I've met cosplayers from all over the world. I've realised that there is just something very precious inside of us all, and that something makes it very easy to create new friendships and have fun together, even if we may not share the same language.'

It's not only the ability to travel and make new friends that Elffi has benefited from through cosplay. 'When I started my hobby as a cosplayer I was really skinny,' he says. 'I've gained around 20 kg (45 lb) of weight since then by following an intensive gym programme, which I developed myself. That's one of the things I love about cosplay: I actually got fit and more healthy because of it!'

Elffi as Jecht from *Final Fantasy*.

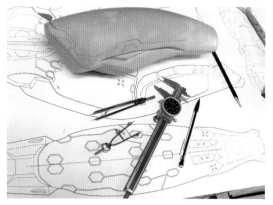

The building of a Needler gun from the video game series *Halo*.

I won't say it's easy money. I definitely made more cash with less time spent when I worked my old graphic design job. But I do make my living building space guns and I have enough cash to pay all my bills and still buy fun stuff for myself every now and again too. Can't really ask for more than that.

Harrison Krix

MAKER

Harrison Krix used to be a graphic designer, but now he spends his time crafting replica rifles, swords, shields and axes. 'My first foray into all this was in 2007, with a few hastily constructed pieces for Halloween.' Not long after, he built a replica Portal Gun from the game of the same name and posted some images of it online. Soon, Krix was getting emails from people asking him to make props for them on commission.

'If I were to apply a label to my job I think "prop maker" would be the most appropriate one. It also speaks to my motivation in the work I do. I'd rather make cool accessories and weapons than whole costumes.' Today, Krix runs his own business, Volpin Props, and has a world of experience to draw on; he knows which materials work best in which applications, which glues are ideal for certain plastics and which paints don't work on particular surfaces and why. This expertise doesn't just allow him to complete his projects faster, but also to do it with more detail and more complexity.

In spite of the increasing use of technology like computer scanning and 3-D printers, Krix says the essence of his craft will always be the relationship between a builder and their basic materials. 'The nice thing about wood and plastic is the accessibility,' he says. 'Anyone can get a $100 scroll saw and a $12 sheet of wood and knock out a space gun in a few weeks, and that's enough to get people hooked. If there's ever a robot invented that can paint and weather a prop better than I can, I'll be concerned, but for now we're just getting access to fantastic tools. You still need to be an artist to make proper use of them.'

Volpin Props has quickly grown into something of a prestige 'brand' in the cosplay scene; Krix is now courted to create accessories not just for cosplayers but film-makers, TV networks and video game companies as well. 'It isn't easy to pull off, as typically I work ten-to-twelve-hour days, every day of the week,' he says. 'I can definitely say this sort of career path isn't for everyone. I like to tell people that my new job is twice the work hours for about the same pay as my old job, and I wouldn't trade back for anything.'

Knightmage

COSPLAYER

'As far as charities and fundraisers go, I've done it all,' says cosplayer Knightmage. Whether it's children's hospital visits, cancer fundraising events or even birthday parties, he's been there, done that, and done it in costume. After realising he felt torn between attending conventions and doing charity events, he came up with an idea. 'Not even Superman can be everywhere at once,' he says. 'People always asked if I sold prints of my costumes, so I thought: how about doing a prints-for-charity campaign?'

At convention appearances he gives out cosplay photo prints for free, but at the same time gives fans the option to donate any amount they like to a variety of charities. 'I think it's a win-win for everyone involved,' Knightmage says. 'On a personal level, I remember how I felt as a kid, seeing my favourite heroes standing in front of me. It didn't matter who was under the mask, all I saw was that bat symbol on the chest.'

Even today, Knightmage says he still gets goosebumps at conventions when he sees people in costume. 'I believe wholeheartedly that superheroes can serve as an inspiration to both the young generation and the old,' he says. 'And cosplayers are the ones in the position to take it to the next level by bringing those heroes to life.'

Eric Ng

PHOTOGRAPHER

With those crowded hallways, ugly carpets and fluorescent lighting, shooting at conventions is hardly ideal. Nevertheless, 'Cosplay hallway shots are very important,' says Eric Ng. 'I began with them years ago and they really allowed me to be comfortable with meeting and talking to people who I wasn't able to approach before.'

Ng starting going to conventions around the age of nine. His dad would take him to smaller cons at first, but they eventually made it to the bigger ones, like Anime Expo and Comic-Con. He'd always had a point-and-shoot, but in 2003 Ng got his first proper digital camera. Two years later, a friend introduced him to the world of private cosplay photo shoots, a world far removed from the crowded convention floors he was used to. 'Little by little,' says Ng, 'I started to get more submerged into the culture and, since then, have made many friends from all over the world.'

Though they are a convention staple, Ng says hallway shoots are artistically limiting. 'It's very difficult to be able to isolate a character and make them unique if you're always faced with a crowd behind them or a convention hall as the backdrop,' he says. 'After three or four years at the same convention, there are only so many places you can reuse before it's recognisable.' This is why he prefers what he calls 'immersive environmental portraiture' – in other words, venturing out to some truly stunning locales. Whether it's travelling through rainforests, across arid deserts or up snowy mountains, Ng and his cosplaying colleagues are always trying to get that perfect pic. 'I've been very spoiled by having friends who have the same drive as I do to travel in order to get shots,' says Ng. 'I owe them everything for their commitment and dedication.'

MrDustinn as Saber from the series *Fate/stay night*.

MrDustinn as Naruto.

Akusesu of Strawberry Censor as Akira Kazama from the fight game series *Rival Schools*.

A2ki of Strawberry Censor as Illyasviel von Einzbern from the spin-off manga and animated series *Fate/kaleid liner Prisma Illya*.

The cosplayer is really the front-facing part of the work. It's like that in all photography: a lot more people are talking about how hot this or that celebrity looked on the cover of *Harper's* than who shot that cover.

Anna Fischer

PHOTOGRAPHER

'At first, photography was just a way for me to produce an image, but over time I was seduced by the medium itself,' says Anna Fischer, who didn't start taking photos until 2008, let alone cosplay images. 'Photography is less immediate and process-oriented than most mediums so it can feel mechanical. But it's got a lot of layers, and you can go pretty deep into its well of possibility.'

Fischer's work goes beyond simply taking beautiful images of costumes. She's able to photograph a model in a way that transforms them, bringing not just an outfit but the character itself to life. It's her ability to capture them at ease that helps make her work stand out. 'Instead of trying to impose my vision on the world, I'm always thinking, "What is the light doing now?" There is a receptive sensitivity, almost a softness, in how I photograph.'

Fischer is so good at what she does she's able to make a living out of it, though the lifestyle isn't exactly rock 'n' roll: 'Most people aren't that eager to sign up for a life of eating cereal twice a day . . .'. While cosplay is gaining more recognition as an art form, opportunities to make a living photographing it are still extremely limited. So what keeps her going back for more? 'I get asked this question the most, and honestly I never have a good answer for it. I could cite issues of identity, and beauty. The malleability of youth culture and the appeal of being someone else. But cosplay and fan culture is where I come from, it's part of me now.'

Anna Fischer

Dandelion's Wish as Hikaru Shidou from the manga series *Magic Knight Rayearth*.

Dandelion's Wish as Mitsuki Koyana from the manga series *Full Moon o Sagashite*.

Linda Le as Rei Ayanami from *Neon Genesis Evangelion*.

MangaFreak150 as Cheza from the anime *Wolf's Rain*.

Vishavjit Singh

COSPLAYER

Unlike most in the cosplay world, Vishavjit Singh didn't get into it for the love of a character. He didn't even know what the word 'cosplay' meant until he Googled it. Instead, he got into cosplay to make a statement.

In 2013, in an exercise aimed at challenging people's stereotypes, Singh, a Sikh, wore a Captain America costume around New York City for a day. Needless to say, reactions were mixed. 'The worst moments were when a few young men hurled verbal abuse my way calling me "Terrorist" and "Captain Arab"," Singh says. But they were isolated blemishes on a day he says was otherwise 'magical'. 'Unexpectedly, I felt like a celebrity given the response of New Yorkers and tourists. The level of attention I got was overwhelming – in a good way. Hundreds if not thousands captured me on their cameras.'

Since then, and following appearances in a magazine article and on a video online, Singh's thoughts on cosplay have changed. From not even knowing what the word meant, he now says: 'I am open to cosplaying again. There's nothing like starting a conversation by shattering stereotypes.'

Directory

Cosplayers

A2ki
facebook.com/StrawberryCensor

Aicosu
aicosu.com

Akira Konomi
worldcosplay.net/member/akira

Akusesu
facebook.com/Akusesu.Cosplay

Allegriana
facebook.com/TheChainmailChick

Allen Amis
allenamiscreations.com

Alodia Gosiengfiao
alodiagosiengfiao.com

Ariana Barouk
arianabarouk.com

Ashley Gosiengfiao
ashlili.com

Ashley Riot
thequeenriot.tumblr.com

Boomie
facebook.com/StrawberryCensor

Chaka Cumberbatch
facebook.com/
PrincessMentalityCosplay

Courtney Morelock
courtoon.deviantart.com

Crabcat Industries
crabcatindustries.com

Crystal Graziano
facebook.com/crystalcosfx

Dandelion's Wish
facebook.com/pages/
Dandelionswishs-
Cosplay/328622393849896

Danny Kelley
facebook.com/kalandkara

Danquish
danquish.deviantart.com

Ed Hoff
facebook.com/EdoSeijin

GG
facebook.com/StrawberryCensor

Giorgia
giorgiacosplay.com

Goldy
gadgettool.web.fc2.com

HezaChan
hezachan.com

Janne 'Elffi' Rusanen
facebook.com/ElffiCosplay

Jia Jem
jiajem.com

Jibrii Ransom
facebook.com/Spectra.Marvelous

Johnny Zabate
junkerscosplay.blogspot.co.uk

Jonathan Carroll
facebook.com/actorjonathancarroll

Julian Checkley
facebook.com/julescheckley

Julie Hagopian
5thny.org

Kamui
kamuicosplay.com

Karen Schnaubelt
costume-con.org

Knightmage
facebook.com/Knightmage1

Laura Jansen
mycosplayfun.tumblr.com

Leon Chiro
leonchirocosplayart.deviantart.com

Linda Le
vampybit.me

Lindze Merritt
lindze.com

Little Wren
facebook.com/LittleWrenLynette

Lyz Brickley
LyzBrickley.com

M. Doc Geressy
carolinaghostbusters.com

MangaFreak150
facebook.com/
MangaFreak150Cosplay

Margie Cox
facebook.com/pages/Margie-
Cox/141429712591364

Maria Rivera
facebook.com/PrimetimeQueen

Meagan Marie
meagan-marie.com

Mei Wai
weibo.com/meiwainevan

Mel Hoppe
windofthestars.com

Meredith Placko
meredithplacko.com

Mo Meinhart
momeinhart.com

Mostflogged
mostflogged.com

MrDustinn
facebook.com/mrdustinn

Nadleeh
meltyylove.blog138.fc2.com

Namiko101
namiko101.deviantart.com

Natalia Voroninsky
alberti.deviantart.com

Nebulaluben
nebulaluben.com

Omi Gibson
kero.dyndns.tv/hp

Paul Tofani
5thny.org

Peter Kokis
brooklynrobotworks.com

Princess Bee
theprincessbee.deviantart.com

Rana McAnear
ranamcanear.com

Rick Boer
rbf-productions-nl.deviantart.com

Shina
facebook.com/ShinaCosplay

Simon Melmeth
501scg.com

Tasha
facebook.com/Spcats.Official.Page

Tham
samuchancosplay.blogspot.co.uk

Thea Teufel
facebook.com/KagomeChansCosplay

Thunderbolt
facebook.com/PixelThunderbolt

Vishavjit Singh
sikhtoons.com

Vitaliya Abramova
facebook.com/kaikida

Yasemin Arslan
facebook.com/yaseminarslan.official

Yaya Han
yayahan.com

Photographers

A. G. Vask
facebook.com/A.G.Vask

Aileen Luib
aileenluibphotography.com

Alison Rose
pixelettephoto.com

Andrew Ho
andrewdhphotos.com

Andrew Michael Phillips
andrewmichaelphillips.com

Anna Fischer
wildplacesproject.com

Benjamin 'Beethy' Koelewijn
beethy.deviantart.com

Benjamin Schwarz
facebook.com/benjamin.schwarz.169

Benn Robbins
robbins-studios.com

Beth Brown
babseyes.com

Bill Rhodes
billrhodesphoto.com

Boris Duval
boristyle.book.fr

Calssara
calssara.com

Cesare Marino
flickr.com/people/sadmanphoto

Chocoball Mukai
namacyoko.blog122.fc2.com

Cozpho Photography
cozpho.deviantart.com

Cynthia Veekens
merdahn.com

Darkain
photoblog.darkain.com

Darrell Ardita
bgzstudios.com

Darshelle Stevens
darshellestevensphotography.com

Eric Ng
bigwhitebazooka.com

Erwin Scheiböck
facebook.com/es.photografie

Eurobeat Kasumi Photography
facebook.com/pages/Eurobeat-
Kasumi-Photography/181144498573739

Fiona Aboud
fionaaboud.com

Girls of the Con / Chaos
Web Productions
girlsofthecon.com

Hell or High Water Photography
hellorhighwaterphotography.
tumblr.com

Hemlep Fotografie
HemlepFotografie.de

Ian Barnard
iantravisbarnard.com

Isshi
cosp.jp/prof.aspx?id=278655

Jakob Schwarz
jakobschwarz.blogspot.de

James J. Barnett
jamesjbarnett.com

Jay Tablante
jaytablante.deviantart.com

Jesús Clares
jesusclares.es

Joe Salcedo / ANOVOS
Productions LLC
anovos.com

Judith Stephens
chohoview.com

Kamil Krawczak
kamilkrawczak.com

Kamil Kurylonek
kurnikoff.com

Kyle Johnsen
cosplay.com

LJinto
flickr.com/photos/ljinto

Lucky Bronson
facebook.com/luckybronson

MAKE
makezine.com

Matt Zeher
zeherfoto.com

Melissa Hammack
facebook.com/MHammackPhotos

Meng
xingyun.cn/luanmengjie

ooxo
ooxo2.exblog.jp

O-show
youtube.com/user/HPLxOShow

Pete Green
petegreenphotography.com

Richie dela Merced
flickr.com/people/14528141@N04

Ron Miller
black-cat-studios.com

Ryohei Takanashi
ryoheitakanashi.tumblr.com

Sarah Hillier
facebook.com/
SarahHillierPhotography

Shashin Kaihi Photography
facebook.com/
ShasinKaihiPhotography

TJ Reynolds
tjrpictures.500px.com

Wenbin Photo
facebook.com/wenbin.photo

Wesley Smith / The Portrait Dude
theportraitdude.com

William Phan
facebook.com/thewillbox

Xenia Rogutenok
rogutenok.deviantart.com

Zan
poro-poro.com

Zhang Jingna
zhangjingna.com

Makers

Bill Doran
props.punishedpixels.com

Harrison Krix
volpinprops.com

Ryo Okita
gyakuyoga.hobby-web.net

Shawn Thorsson
protagonist4hire.blogspot.co.uk

Others

Bruce Mai
costume.org

International Costumers' Guild
costume.org

Nobuyuki Takahashi
hard.co.jp

Pierre Pettinger
costume.org

Tess Fowler
tessfowler.com

Yoshiyuki Matsunaga
cospa.com

Picture Credits

Acknowledgements

We would like to thank: Our editor Ali Gitlow for making this project happen, Aimee Selby and Lincoln Dexter for their tireless work. Ron Miller. Bruce Mai, Pierre Pettinger and everyone at the International Costumers' Guild. Karen Schnaubelt. Jay Tablante. Meagan Marie. Julian Checkley. Judith Stephens. Sang Kwon, Eric Jou. Ed Hoff, Akira Konomi, Stephen Totilo, Kotaku and Gawker Media.

Brian would like to thank: Shoko, Ren, Louis and Ewan. Mom and Dad. The Ueda Family. Jerry Martinez and Rolling Thunder Pictures.

Luke would like to thank: Mel, Annabel, William, Mum and Dad and Emily. And the Melvins.

Thank you to all the cosplayers, makers and photographers who contributed to this book, as well as cosplayers and photographers everywhere.

© Prestel Verlag, Munich · London · New York, 2014
© for the text by Brian Ashcraft and Luke Plunkett, 2014
© for the photographs see Picture Credits, 2014

Front cover: Ariana Barouk as Silk Spectre from the
graphic novel *Watchmen*, photo by Jay Tablante
Back cover: Danny Kelley as Superman, photo by
Andrew Michael Phillips

Prestel Verlag, Munich
A member of Verlagsgruppe Random House GmbH

Prestel Verlag
Neumarkter Strasse 28
81673 Munich
Tel. +49 (0)89 4136-0
Fax +49 (0)89 4136-2335

www.prestel.de

Prestel Publishing Ltd.
14–17 Wells Street
London W1T 3PD
Tel. +44 (0)20 7323-5004
Fax +44 (0)20 7323-0271

Prestel Publishing
900 Broadway, Suite 603
New York, NY 10003
Tel. +1 (212) 995-2720
Fax +1 (212) 995-2733

www.prestel.com

Library of Congress Control Number: 2014936644

British Library Cataloguing-in-Publication Data: a
catalogue record for this book is available from the British
Library; Deutsche Nationalbibliothek holds a record of this
publication in the Deutsche Nationalbibliografie; detailed
bibliographical data can be found under: http://dnb.d-nb.de

Prestel books are available worldwide. Please contact
your nearest bookseller or one of the above addresses for
information concerning your local distributor.

Editorial direction: Ali Gitlow
Editorial assistance: Lincoln Dexter
Copyediting and proofreading: Aimee Selby
Chinese translation: Eric Jou
Korean translation: Sang Kwon (Zero Rock Entertainment)

Design and layout: Bags of Joy
Production: Friederike Schirge
Origination: Reproline Mediateam, Munich
Printing and binding: Printer Trento

Printed in Italy

ISBN 978-3-7913-4925-1

Verlagsgruppe Random House FSC® N001967
The FSC® -certified paper Profisilk has been supplied by
Igepa, Germany